Technology and Competition in the Brazilian Computer Industry

Technology and Competition in the Brazilian Computer Industry

Paulo Bastos Tigre

St. Martin's Press, New York

Library of Congress Cataloging in Publication Data
Tigre, Paul Bastos.
   Technology and competition in the Brazilian computer industry.
   Bibliography: p.
   1. Computer industry—Brazil. 2. Technology transfer.
I. Title.
HD9696.C63B78   1983   338.8'200164'0981   82-21487
ISBN 0-312-78787-1

CONTENTS

FOREWORD

Since the days of Friedrich List, the question of 'infant industries' has preoccupied economists. List argued that the development of 'intellectual capital' was fundamental to the development process and criticized Adam Smith for his failure to give sufficient weight to the problems of accumulating technical know-how and skills at all levels of the labour force. Adam Smith had argued that it was wasteful and unnecessary 'artificially' to promote new industries by state intervention and quoted the hypothetical example of wine-making in Scotland. List ridiculed this example and in connection with the industries already established argued that Adam Smith 'falsely maintains that these manufactures have originated in the natural course of things and of their own accord; notwithstanding that in every nation the political power interferes to give to this so-called natural course an artificial direction for the nation's own special advantage'. He argued furthermore that those nations which had fallen behind in the competitive struggle should systematically seek to foster new technology and to improve upon those technologies which they were obliged to import.

The countries of Latin America have increasingly confronted these very basic issues of industrial development and nowhere more than in Brazil is this debate still relevant today. The 'dependency' school have pointed (as List did) to the extreme difficulties confronting developing countries as they attempt to compete with the powerful established leaders in world technology. The case of the Brazilian computer industry is therefore of quite exceptional interest throughout the world. Paulo Tigre has made an extremely valuable contribution to our understanding of the wider issues through his careful and original study of this industry. I am very happy that his work in the Science Policy Research Unit at Sussex has led to such a useful contribution to this literature.

Christopher Freeman
Sussex
August 1982

ACKNOWLEDGEMENTS

I am very grateful to Dr Ed Sciberras whose guidance, encouragement and friendship have been invaluable. He advised me in every stage of the work, making a strong contribution to my understanding of the issues involved in the study.

A number of other people have played a significant role in encouraging the project. I wish to express my gratitude to my father Helios Bastos Tigre who collected important material for the book, to Dr Ivan da Costa Marques who first introduced me to the computer industry, to Charlotte Huggett who helped me to make the book readable, to Linda Gardiner for her skill and dedication in typing the manuscript and to the people who read and commented on all or part of the earlier versions of the book—Vitoria Tigre, Tom Price, Charles Cooper, Renelson Sampaio, Norman Clark, Joao Carlos Ferraz, Francisco Teixeira and Quazi Ahmed. I am also indebted to the individuals and organizations, too numerous to mention, who assisted me during my field work overseas. For financial support I am grateful to acknowledge a grant from the Brazilian Council for Science and Technology Development (CNPQ).

LIST OF ABBREVIATIONS

Abicomp	Brazilian Computer Industry Association
BNDE	National Economic Development Bank
BSC	Binary Synchronous Code
Capre	Electronic Data Processing Activities Coordination (Ministry of Planning)
CDC	Control Data Corporation
CII	Companie International D'Informatique
CKD	Completely Knocked Down
Cobra	Computadores e Sistemas Brasileiros SA
CPU	Central Processing Unit
CRT	Cathode Ray Tube
DEC	Digital Equipment Corporation
Digibras	Empresa Digital Brasileira SA
DN	*Datanews*
DP	Data Processing
ECLA	Economic Commission for Latin America (United Nations)
EDB	Eletronica Digital Brasileira
Edisa	Eletronica Digital SA
EDP	Electronic Data Processing
EEC	European Economic Commission
FDI	Foreign Direct Investment
Finame	BNDE's Fund for Locally Manufactured Capital Goods Financing
FT	*Financial Times*
HP	Hewlett Packard
IBCT	Industria Brasileira de Capsulas Telefonicas
IBM	International Business Machines
ICL	International Computers Limited
INPI	Industrial Propriety National Institute
IOF	Financial Operations Tax
JV	Joint Ventures
KB	Kylo (1000) bytes
LDC	Less Developed Country
LSI	Large Scale Integration

MB	Mega (1 000 000) bytes
MNC	Multinational Corporation
MSI	Medium Scale Integration
NCE	Nucleo Computacao Eletronica (UFRJ)
NCR	National Cash Register
NIC	Newly Industrialized Country
OECD	Organization for Economic Cooperation and Development
OEM	Original Equipment Manufacturer
POS	Point-of-Sale Terminal
Procergs	Data Processing Company of the State of Rio Grande do Sul
PUC	Pontifical Catholic University
R & D	Research and Development
SBC	Brazilian Computer Society
SEI	Special Secretary for Informatics
Serpro	Federal Data Processing Service
SID	Sistemas de Informacao Distribuida SA
SKD	Semi-Knocked Down
SLT	Solid Logic Technology
SNA	Systems Network Architecture
SRT	Special Representative for Trade Negotiations (US Government)
Sucesu	Computer Users Society
UFMG	Minas Gerais Federal University
UFRGS	Rio Grande Do Sul Federal University
UFRJ	Rio De Janeiro Federal University
US	United States
USP	University of São Paulo
VDU	Video Display Unit
VLSI	Very Large Scale Integration
WO	Wholly Owned

INTRODUCTION

The issue of industrialization in developing countries has been a major preoccupation of development economists in recent years. The difficulties and opportunities faced by developing countries in acquiring technical capability and autonomously developing new branches of the industry have been a source of controversy.

The possibilities of autonomous industrial development in the periphery are viewed pessimistically by the dependency school.[1] Within the school, the more orthodox Marxian authors are the most sceptical about the prospects for capitalist development in the periphery. For example, Frank (1978) and Santos (1973) argue that capitalist development, or at least autonomous capitalist development, is not possible in the periphery because of its subservient role within the international economy. Amin (1978) and Marini (1972b) reached similar conclusions. They described a peripheral model based on low wage exports and dominated by multinational corporations (MNCs). Under these conditions they saw no possibility of transition to a self-centred system based on production of mass-consumption and capital goods.

Cardoso (1979) who is usually identified as *'dependentista'* does not recognize limits on industrial development at the periphery at the general theoretical level. He insists on the need to analyse particular situations rather than to develop general theories. However, Cardoso does emphasize that accumulation and expansion of capital cannot find its essential dynamic component within the periphery itself because of the absence of capital goods and financial sectors, the import of technology and penetration by foreign multinationals.

There has been more fundamental criticism of the dependency theory by economists such as Warren (1973), Lall (1980) and Soete (1981). One of the main arguments is that capitalism is developing in many parts of the periphery. The growth of the newly industrialized countries (NICs) such as Brazil, Argentina, Mexico, South Korea, Taiwan, Hong Kong and Singapore is used to suggest that

[1] The origin of the dependency school is usually attributed to the United Nations Economic Commission for Latin America (ECLA) and to the Marxian and neo-Marxian North Americans (Baran, Sweezy and Frank).

there may be important benefits of international integration for peripheral economies. Included among the benefits are the continued access to developed economy markets and to international finance and technology.

There is substantial evidence supporting the idea that international integration can stimulate the periphery's industrialization through the reallocation of production, development of new market channels and flow of capital and technical information. But an economy which is heavily dependent on foreign capital and technology and oriented towards the export market is potentially vulnerable to changes and fluctuations in the international economy. For example, in the early 1980s most NICs had their access to markets eroded by protectionism. Furthermore, their access to credit was reduced by the resultant doubts about the ability of the debtor nations to meet their growing commitments.

Recently, the issue of technology appears to have replaced development and growth problems as the central concern in the dependency controversy. The dependency view may be summarized by Cardoso (1973) who maintained that 'in spite of internal economic development, countries tied to international capitalism by that type of linkage remain economically dependent, insofar as the production of technology is concentrated in advanced capitalist economies.'

A critic of dependency, Lall (1980), gathered evidence on the generation of technology by indigenous enterprises in the poorer countries. Many developing countries have in fact become exporters of technology, sometimes including turn-key industrial plants and engineering services. Katz (1982) also recognizes the possibilities of some developing countries achieving a relative technological independence based on the transfer of technological designs originated abroad. The evidence shows that local technological capabilities in developing countries have been underestimated. This underestimation has partly been a result of the influence of 'marginalization' arguments which lead to the *a priori* conclusion that innovation, technological adaptations and skills required for them are absent in Third World economies (Cooper and Hoffman, 1978), by virtue of being peripheral to the mainstream of international economic activity. According to Soete (1981), to the extent that technology is essentially a dynamic concept, dependency does not seem to be the appropriate framework to analyse technological dependencies.

Although it may have inadequacies as *the* framework of analysis for the technology problem in developing countries, the dependency theory has made important contributions to the understanding of how dominant relationship is developed and maintained by developed countries through international trade and investment. This involves the exercise of monopolistic market power by MNCs in developing countries, preventing indigenous firms from entering their own home market, the role of technology imports in inhibiting local research and development (R & D) efforts and foreign control over licensing agreements which may prevent a real transfer of technology to the Third World.

In developing countries, MNCs usually establish activities such as assembling and testing which are cheap-labour intensive. R & D activities are mainly restricted to their parent countries or subsidiaries in other developed countries. This has several important implications for the Third World economy. First, any job creation is oriented towards low-paid manual work. Although some qualified personnel are used in technical support, administrative and marketing activities, subsidiaries of MNCs seldom employ local people to perform high-level technical functions such as product design and engineering. Consequently, local industry is deprived of the sorts of skills which could exploit the establishment of significant links with local universities and research centres. Secondly, dependence on foreign sources of technology has negative economic implications in the mid and long term. The simple importation of product and process specifications which could otherwise possibly be developed locally can hinder the development of an R & D industry, waste scarce foreign currency and encourage the use of imported components and capital goods in manufacture. Thirdly, foreign technology is sometimes inadequate and inappropriate for local needs.

The growth of a high-technology industry in a large developing country is obviously a particularly relevant experience to examine in the attempt to understand the problem of developing technology in Third World countries. It is intended that this study of the computer industry in Brazil contributes to this understanding.

The development of industrial technology in developing countries depends on both favourable macroeconomic and microeconomic conditions (Katz, 1982). Macroeconomic conditions are influenced by broad economic policies rather than by specific industrial policies and therefore are not under the scope of this study. Microeconomic variables which influence innovative activities include the nature of the product technology, the characteristics and size of the market, the relationship with the foreign supplier of technology, the local availability of skilled engineers and scientists to undertake R & D activities and the degree of protection enjoyed by local technology.

The development of the computer industry in Brazil depended upon a number of favourable conditions, some of the most important of which were created artificially by the government and not by the operation of free market forces.

The introduction of the microprocessor in the early 1970s had an important impact on the structure of the computer industry worldwide. Very dense integrated circuits and microprocessors incorporating the bulk of the electronic technology required by complex computer systems replaced transistors which characterized the earlier second computer generation. This gave the opportunity for new entry in the highly concentrated computer market not only in the USA but also in Europe and Japan. Since such devices can be purchased from independent suppliers, small new firms with ingenious design teams achieved tremendous success developing products incorporating the new technology. This is well illustrated in the case of Apple Computer Inc. The firm was established in the mid-seventies. It was initially installed in the garage of one of its younger founders. Only six years later Apple was already one of the pacesetters in the world microcomputer market with sales of US $335 million by 1981.

Successful entry in the mainstream computer industry requires large-scale product development and market support. This includes technical assistance, customer financing and the development of application software. These activities require heavy capital investment and the building-up of business practices based on a long-term process of learning-by-doing.

Although the characteristics of computer *technology* offers opportunities for new market entry, the nature of the computer *market* does not encourage new ventures. The computer market is highly concentrated. Existing manufacturers such as IBM which holds more than half of the computer market worldwide enjoy goodwill, cost advantages and have a well established marketing network. These are expensive to establish and impossible to duplicate in the short term.

Relationship with the foreign supplier of technology is important. Licensing agreements can include clauses giving power to foreign licensers to control local licensees' logistic and strategic decisions. Possible types of control are export restrictions, product selection, choice of manufacturing techniques and equipment, and procurement policy. Licensers' control over such decisions can limit licensees' opportunities to absorb effectively and further develop the licensed technology.

Local availability of skilled scientists and engineers to perform R & D activities is of fundamental importance to the development of the computer industry. The foreign computer firms which supplied the Brazilian market trained local engineers and technicians to perform customers' support activities and to develop some application software. But as they did not operate R & D activities in Brazil they were unable to train local professional manpower to perform activities such as system software and hardware design and development.

Finally, the development of technology in Third World countries requires protection against a free import of designs from abroad. From the point of view of an individual firm in a developing country it is easier and less risky to import already proven designs and components from abroad than to develop them in-house. As Lall (1982) said:

Where the free inflow of technology is permitted, either by direct foreign investment or by passive reliance on continuous licensing, the local capability to acquire know-how develops more slowly.

In Brazil many firms perceived the opportunities offered by the new microelectronic technology and successfully designed and developed products based on microprocessors. Some firms quickly acquired foreign technology through the use of licensing agreements. However, they face several difficulties. These include the problem of maintaining technological development with limited resources while facing direct or indirect competition from large foreign multinationals.

Brazil ranks between seventh and tenth in the world computer market. Sales of data-processing equipment by Brazilian-owned firms grew twelvefold between 1978 and 1981, climbing from US $30 million to US $400 million. However, the prospect for local firms may not be as bright as the growth figures may imply. The cost of recent programmes in manufacturing marketing and R & D, in a situation of severe financial constraints, has increased firms' dependence on short-term external financing. There are thirteen firms involved in developing and manufacturing microcomputers locally. Such a large number of firms in the market not only hardens competitive conditions but may jeopardize the chances of fostering the creation of a large internationally competitive Brazilian computer firm. Brazilian data-processing equipment manufacturers may therefore be too numerous to be justified by the size of the market.

In the Brazilian computer industry many licensees appear to have succeeded in retaining a considerable degree of freedom concerning technological decisions. Another positive factor was the availability in local university and research centres of high-level engineers to design and develop some types of computer products.

In Brazil the creation of an independent computer industry was favoured by government intervention. The government has regulated imports and restricted direct manufacturing by MNCs in order to reserve the most dynamic segments of the computer industry (micro and minicomputers) to Brazilian-owned manufacturers. Regulations concerning technology transfer agreements (including ato normativo no. 15—INPI) have reduced packaging and control practices since they explicitly ban most types of restrictive clauses in licensing agreements. Also, the government bodies in charge of computer policy in Brazil (SEI and Digibras) have attempted to exclude packaging and restrictive operations by advising local firms in negotiations with foreign technology suppliers and by themselves refusing permission to projects involving control by licensers. To a lesser extent the government has provided protection for local technology developments. This included turning down projects utilizing foreign technology in areas where there were local design capabilities such as microcomputers, low-speed modems and bank terminals.

The main aim of this work is to explore the process of developing computer technology in Brazil—and in particular to examine the connection between technology strategies and competitive behaviour of firms. The work is in two parts: the first theoretical, the other empirical and analytical.

Part One reviews the literature relevant to major theoretical problem areas. Some hypotheses are raised deriving from unresolved and conflicting positions in recent literature on the theory of the firm and technology transfer.

Chapter One looks at the issue of the process of concentration and internationalization of capital and its implications for developing countries. Chapter Two discusses the policies of MNCs towards ownership and control of overseas subsidiaries. Chapter Three discusses the question of comparative advantages in producing technology. Chapter Four focuses on licensing agreements with particular emphasis on the attitudes of MNCs to the sale of technology and the reasons for acquiring technology through licensing agreements. It also identifies major technological strategies of the individual firm. Chapter Five reviews recent studies of the control mechanism utilized by technology suppliers and the implications for strategic decision-making in licensed firms.

Part Two includes an analysis of the Brazilian computer industry.

Chapter Six provides some factual background information on the industry. This includes definitions of data-processing equipment and assessment of the size of the market in Brazil. It also includes an outline of the industry structure, state computer policy and the development of Brazilian firms design capabilities. Chapter Seven analyses the competitive behaviour of Brazilian computer firms. Chapter Eight focuses on technology strategies, including R & D, licensing and the utilization of locally manufactured components. Chapter Nine examines the entry strategies of computer MNCs in Brazil. Chapter Ten evaluates the nature and extent of control and packaging practices in licensing agreements between Brazilian and foreign computer firms. Chapter Eleven draws together the major conclusions of the study, with respect to foreign investment and barriers to entry, joint ventures and ownership policies and technology transfer and development.

RESEARCH METHODS

The study attempts to obtain empirical answers to particular analytical hypotheses drawn from economic theory. It does not attempt to develop elaborate models or 'complete' theories. A complex model appropriate for one industrial sector or national economy may be inappropriate for another sector or country. On the other hand, less ambitious, more simple, hypothesis may be relevant, in particular for other developing countries which have reached similar stages of import substitution industrialization and for other technologically oriented industries which operate under a similar international oligopolistic market structure.

The research involved 40 in-depth interviews (31 in Brazil, 5 in the USA, 2 in West Germany, one in Britain and one in France), review of published material and the sending of 19 questionnaires by mail.

Although the sample of firms was largely representative (accounting for about 90 per cent of the sales of DP equipment in Brazil in 1980) it is necessary to recognize the limitation of the interview as a research method. One limitation is the likely tendency of respondents to exaggerate the technical and commercial achievements of their firms and present over optimistic prospects as far as technology autonomy is concerned. However, in this study, reliability was safeguarded by the adoption of the following techniques:

1 In seven cases, *both* partners (licensers and licensees) in licensing agreements were interviewed. This enabled cross-checking of responses and sharpened the reliability of information about the arrangements undertaken. Three Brazilian licensees, for example, claimed to enjoy complete freedom concerning the export of licensed products, while

licensers admitted that their licensing agreements included unwritten export prohibition to specific countries or a ban on all exports.

2   Often responses from firms were compared with information obtained from government officials. Although the latter officially avoided releasing confidential data about specific firms, they were able to provide useful information about the technological performance of major indigenous manufacturers. Questionnaire responses were also compared with information from published material such as industry journals.

3   Whenever possible the questionnaires were presented to more than one manager in the same area and in other areas within the firm.

4   Questionnaire results were statistically correlated. This enabled the identification of contradictions between technological strategies and competitive behaviour of firms. These were subject to further checking and analysis. For example, firms which claimed to have technical capabilities as a major competitive advantage had other technological-related indicators cross-checked. These included, number of employees in R & D as compared with total personnel, R & D expenditure as a percentage of sales and source of technology and characteristics of the firms' product line.

The statistical method utilized in the various analyses was Yules' Q bivariate correlations. It gives correlation coefficients varying from -1 to 1 for the relationship between variables collapsed into dichotomous categories, such as: yes or no, large or small, etc. Correlations are thought to be significant when $Q > 0.6$.

The correlation coefficients obtained were subjected to a further statistical test—tne chi-square test (χ^2). It evaluated whether or not coefficients obtained empirically by Yules' Q differ significantly from those which would be expected under a certain set of theoretical assumptions.

The statistical results do not of course claim to prove the hypothesis. They were, however, found to lend support to the qualitative findings obtained in the interviews and discussions.

PART ONE

1 INTERNATIONAL OLIGOPOLY AND BARRIERS TO ENTRY

The application of increasingly sophisticated technology to production has been one of the distinguishing characteristics of economic life since the beginning of the Industrial Revolution. In 1776 Adam Smith formulated the first coherent body of logical explanation for technical advance. He argued that it was based on the division of labour.

The invention of all those machines by which labour is so much facilitated and abridged seems to have been originally owing to the division of labour. Men are much more likely to discover easier and readier methods of attaining any object when the whole attention of their minds is directed towards that single object than when it is dissipated among a great variety of things.

The development of manufacturing technology originated a process of industrial concentration. This was first discussed in Volume I of *Capital*. Marx considered centralization as a historical tendency of capital accumulation.

The expropriation of capitalists by other capitalists is accomplished by the action of the imminent laws of capitalistic production itself, by the centralization of capital. One capitalist always kills many. Hand in hand with this centralization, or this expropriation of many capitalists by few, develop on an ever-extending scale, the co-operative form of the labour process, the conscious technical application of science . . . , the entanglement of all people in the net of the world-market, and, with this, the international character of capitalistic regime.

The study of the consequences of this process on the organization of the firm and market structures has absorbed the attention of an increasing number of economists in recent years. Schumpeter (1939) claimed that the large firm is the most powerful engine of progress and that market concentration is important for technical progress. Galbraith (1967) observed that technical development requires heavy investment of capital, high specialization, division and sub-division of any task into component parts, more time spent on Research and Development (R & D) and long-term planning. Consequently, there is an ever-increasing concentration of production in the hands of large corporations.

Observers like Baratt Brown (1974) have verified that

The process of concentration of production in large firms has accelerated at certain periods—at the turn of the century, in the 1920's, 1940's and 1960's—but there has been little evidence of decentralization in between. The one hundred largest manufacturing corporations in the USA controlled 58 per cent of the land, building and equipment used in manufacturing in 1962 as compared with 44 per cent in 1929.

Stephen Hymer (1972) argued that current trends could result in the domination of two-thirds of world industrial output by 300 or 400 companies. For the British economy, Newbold and Jackson speculated that in the foreseeable future, unless countervailing action is taken, three-quarters of the non-nationalized sector of British industry could be controlled by as few as twenty-one giant companies (Holland, 1975).[1] In the computer industry a single firm (IBM) holds between 60 and 70 per cent of the world market. IBM dominates the sector expected to undergo the greatest development in the coming decades —data processing and data communications. IBM's dominant position in the computer market is driving the firm to control of other markets through vertical integration, from component to satellite (Nora and Minc, 1978).

Sylos-Labini (1956) noted that the process of industrial concentration generates and increases the market power of the largest firms. Oligopoly becomes the most frequent market form of modern economics. As large firms become increasingly international, so oligopolistic structures tend to become international. As prospects in a domestic market become limited, firms turn to exports or to overseas production as means to growth. This process happens to firms in one industry in several developed countries. Consequently, large firms come into contact with each other in the international market creating a worldwide oligopoly.

In newly industrialized countries (NICs) oligopolistic multinational firms dominance is very pronounced in the high-technology industries. In Brazil, for example, foreign participation represents more than 70 per cent of industrial turnover in mechanical engineering, electrical and communication equipment, transport equipment, plastic and pharmaceutical products (Tigre, 1978). In the late 1970s 50 per cent of total assets in manufacturing were owned by multinational firms. Market domination by foreign firms is the result of pioneering local production and the take-over of existing local firms.

There are at least three different explanations for the competitive

[1] Fouad Ajami presents a survey on projections of economic concentration in 'Corporate Giants—Some Global Social Costs', in Modelski, G. (1979).

advantages of multinational firms *vis-à-vis* national firms in developing countries.

The conventional explanation derives from the theory of industrial organization. Industrial concentration is considered as a natural process of reorganizing resources towards greater efficiency. Johnson (1970), for example, saw this dominance as a reflection of comparative advantages. Accordingly the multinational corporations (MNCs) possess superior technology, permitting greater efficiency and thus greater profits. Monopoly over technology is seen as a temporary advantage to compensate private investment in knowledge creation. In relation to access to credit, Johnson argues that there is, especially in recent years, a preference among foreign companies for raising as much capital as they can in the local market, thereby competing in that market with domestic companies. He concluded:

The explanation may well be that the comparative advantage of these companies lies in their possession of superior technology rather than in access to a cheaper source of capital than is available to their domestic competitors, and this advantage enables them to raise capital on the same terms as their domestic competitors without impairing their competitive abilities.

In contrast to this view, other recent theories state that the advantage of MNCs does not lie mainly in their greater efficiency, but in various distortions in the international market for technology and capital. According to these theories a necessary condition of direct foreign investment is that the investing firm has some monopolistic advantages.

This was initially proposed in 1960 by Stephen Hymer. Firms engaged in direct investment have monopolistic elements. The advantage of the source-country firms is attributed to proprietary information—patents, know-how—which is not available to host-country firms on equally favourable price and terms.

The development of a new product is a fixed cost; once expenditure needed for invention or innovation has been made, it is forever a bygone. The actual cost of production is thus typically well below selling price and the limit on output is not rising costs but falling demand due to saturated markets. The marginal profit of new foreign markets is thus high and corporations have a strong interest in maintaining a system which spreads their products widely. Thus the interest of MNCs in underdeveloped countries is greater than the size of market would suggest.

Richard Newfarmer (1979b) examined the causes of the growth of foreign dominance in the Brazilian electrical-machinery industry. He confirmed theories of imperfections in the international market for technology. He argued that

. . . if national firms, like MNCs' subsidiaries, could buy technology for a royalty payment equal to the marginal cost of its development, then Brazilian firms would buy technology and raise profits concomitantly . . . The fact that Brazilians cannot buy technology at cost, reflects the MNCs' economic power in the market rather than greater efficiency.

Newfarmer also verified that there is a strong bias in favour of MNCs in the financial markets. Because of their smaller size, local firms usually pay a higher price for finance. In addition, they may suffer disadvantages in both phases of the business cycle. He argues:

In a recession higher interest rates and credit rationing hit smaller firms harder and faster. In a time of dynamic expansion and easy money, small firms cannot expand as rapidly as large firms with access to huge blocks of capital. They may lose their share of market growth.

Many other authors have carried out empirical studies of the oligopolistic role of MNCs. These include the works of Bain (1956), Penrose (1959), Vernon (1966–71), Kindleberger (1970), Caves (1971), Marris (1971), Hirsch (1976), Lall and Streeten (1977) and Guimaraes (1980).

A third explanation of MNCs' competitive advantages over mono-national firms is based on their international scale of operations. Ruthemberg (1972) sees this advantage as a consequence of MNCs' worldwide base. Economies of scale may thus occur in R & D and manufacturing. Marketing activities are facilitated by the possibility of using national markets as test markets for other nations. Multi-national production gives an opportunity to use to the full the law of comparative advantage by dispersing subproducts over several subsidiaries in various countries.

An MNC can maximize its profits by minimizing the sum of taxes it pays worldwide. This can be achieved by reallocating revenue from high-tax nations to low-tax nations through the manipulation of transfer-prices, intersubsidiary loans, managerial fees and royalties. Moreover, an MNC has potential access to all capital markets of the world.

To the extent that the company can move between nations, it can stand aloof from the monetary policy of individual nations and raise capital from the cheapest source anywhere. This gives the MNC a direct cost of capital advantage over a collection of national companies. (Rutenberg, 1972.)

The financial advantages of MNCs have also been studied by Behrman (1970) with similar conclusions—financial power of the parent, the high earnings of the affiliates, the ability to transfer funds among affiliates of the enterprise and the greater ability to tap international financial resources.

Aliber's (1969) explanation of the competitive advantages of MNCs is centred on the advantages of vertical integration and economies of scale.

Certain economic processes have flow characteristics. Efficiencies may be realised by coordinating activities that occur in several different countries within the firm.

Casson's (1979) concept of internationalization is also consistent with this argument. He believes that the advantages of an MNC are based on its facility for transferring resources internationally without exchange of ownership. Consequently, whenever there is an international transaction, MNCs would enjoy gains, compared with local firms. Casson's analysis suggests two types of industries in which internationalization will predominate. The first are industries which rely heavily on proprietary information; the second are industries which operate multistage production processes with increasing returns to scale or with capital-intensive techniques.

The source of competitive advantages of MNCs *vis-à-vis* mononational firms varies according to industrial sector, geographical structure and size of the market, government policies and corporate strategies. One important issue deriving from those advantages is the effect of foreign direct investment (FDI) on national industry's competitiveness. Studies of this fall broadly into two conflicting positions: those which postulate that FDI increases the level of competitiveness in national industries, and those which argue that FDI, especially in developing countries, restrains competition through the erection of barriers to entry for local firms.

Among the economists postulating that FDI increases competition are Behrman, Johnson and Kojima. Behrman (1970) found that PDI goes into technically advanced industries, contributing to the general competitiveness of the host industry, especially in relation to exports. Johnson (1970) argued that the superior performance of foreign firms reduces prices for consumers and contributes to the separation of efficient from inefficient firms. Japanese economist Kiyoshi Kojima (1978) claimed that FDI in developing countries plays the role of a 'tutor'. Gradually, FDI has an effect spread over the specific industry in the host country through the training of shop-floor workers, engineers and managers, and makes the establishment of competitive firms by local capital possible. This ultimately raises the production function of the industry in question and makes the new industries competitive in the international markets.

Conflicting with these theorists are empirical and theoretical researches which support the idea that FDI restrains competition and paves the way for the establishment of barriers to entry for local firms. Stephen Hymer (1972) argued this and that local government should restrict the operation of MNCs in order to establish a certain degree of competition in local industries. Richard Newfarmer (1979) and Eduardo Guimaraes (1980) conducted empirical works on the effects of FDI on the competitiveness of the Brazilian electrical and automobile industries respectively. The former was struck by the rapid denationalization, market concentration and imposition of barriers to entry produced by massive FDI in the sector. Guimaraes found that local firms could not enter their own home market unless the government adopted discriminatory measures against MNCs in order to set limits to their growth.

According to Bain (1956) there are three main sources or types of barriers to entry. They are product differentiation, absolute cost disadvantages and economies of scale.

Product differentiation occurs through various forms of differentiation in terms of price, design, quality standards, marketing structure and customer services. They arise (a) because buyer preferences are established due to goodwill, the effects of brand names, loyalty or simply inertia; (b) from superior product design as a result of the control of patents or simply secret know-how preservation; (c) through the control of distribution outlets when alternative channels of distribution would be costly to establish.

Absolute cost disadvantages exist when the established firms have (a) superior production techniques and know-how which are not available at cost to others; (b) control over, or favourable access to, suppliers of important factor inputs such as raw materials, management and operatives which cannot be obtained from alternative sources at the same price; (c) lower cost of finance.

Economies of scale constitute a barrier where (a) the minimum optimal scale of production represents a large proportion of total industry output; (b) unit costs at a sub-optimal level of output are substantially above those at the optimal output.

These past studies leave the issue of the impact of FDI on competition unresolved. Therefore, with respect to the Brazilian computer industry there are conflicting hypotheses to be examined. (Hyp. 1.1) is that *Direct investment by multinational firms increases competition in national industry through the introduction of foreign technology to the local firms.*

The alternative hypothesis (Hyp. 1.2) is that *Direct investment by multinational firms in developing countries restrains competi-*

tion and imposes oligopolistic barriers to entry for indigenous firms.

The next chapter will review the theoretical discussion on joint ventures and ownership strategies of firms. These issues are relevant to the study of the Brazilian computer industry because of their implication for policy. This includes the relationship between ownership control and technology transfer.

2   JOINT VENTURES AND OWNERSHIP POLICIES

Some countries have in recent years taken steps requiring MNCs to enter partnership with local investors. This policy has been especially implemented in developing countries where the sense of dependence has been felt more acutely. Mexico, Nigeria, India, Pakistan and some South East Asia countries are applying continued pressure on foreign investors for a minimum of local partnership.

Pakistan and India adopted an explicit policy towards joint ventures since their independence in 1947. The *Industrial Policy Statement* published by the government of Pakistan in 1948 stated that Pakistan nationals should have a chance to subscribe at least 30 per cent of the equity in all companies. Since the introduction in January 1974 of the 'Foreign Exchange Regulation Act', India's foreign investment has become highly selective. In general, the government insists that foreign investors enter into joint ventures with Indian enterprises, and equity participation is usually limited to 40 per cent. Majority participation (up to 100 per cent of the equity in exceptional cases) may, however, be granted to enterprises which export a large proportion of their turnover, and those considered essential to India's needs. Tomlinson (1970), who studied the nature of British firms' ownership strategies in India and Pakistan, found that 42.5 per cent entered into joint ventures because of either explicit or implicit host-government pressures.

A typical form of pressure in Mexico is a request by government officials for a 'Mexicanization' plan for companies requesting import permits. In Nigeria two 'indigenizations' decrees have taken Nigerian participation in many foreign companies to 60 per cent. In all, about 1200 companies had to comply with the decrees and the vast majority of them did so through private arrangements.

In South East Asia three countries have taken a 'hard line' on foreign investment in order to ensure local participation. In 1972 the government of Thailand declared that foreigners could no longer own a controlling interest in companies in certain fields. In the Philippines foreign shareholding has been limited to 30 per cent in particular fields, and in Indonesia, where the shortage of local capital has been more severe, it was announced in the late 1970s that 51 per cent of the share of joint-venture companies must be in local hands within ten years (Weinstein, 1979).

The justification for policies that require foreigners to have local partners usually rests on three claims: first, that local ownership will cut down the future outflow of resources from the country; second, that it will increase the local economy's control over the operations of foreign-owned facilities; and third, that it will promote technology transfer by giving local partners access to technical knowledge generated abroad.

Objectives and operations of MNCs in developing countries may not be consistent with the objectives of the host countries. Local government may thus wish to establish some sort of special control over the operations of MNCs. Local partnership, especially a 51 per cent majority holding, is often seen as a major instrument to achieve this control. It is expected that if a local subsidiary has to answer for its actions not only to its foreign parents, but to a substantial minority of shareholders as well, this offers the most effective possible guarantee that the potential conflicts of interest between the objectives of a national economy and those of an international company will be more equitably resolved.

This view is widely found among many economists and executives. A study undertaken by the Conference Board on US multinationals' corporate behaviour in Canada illustrates this. One manager interviewed, reflecting the view of executives in several other companies, said:

The wholly-owned subsidiary cannot maximize decisions in the interests of the host country. Even a minority shareholding interest in the host country builds a countervailing force into the decision-making process of the subsidiary. This is the bare minimum that provide a voice within the firm, within the subsidiary, which speaks for local interests.

This view is not universal, however, and needs to be established. Therefore in the case of the Brazilian computer industry the hypothesis to be studied concerning joint ventures (Hyp. 2.1) is that *A majority local partnership in overseas subsidiaries permits local control over policies and operations. This enables technological transfer through access to technical knowledge generated abroad.*

It has been argued, however, that MNCs often exercise control over operations of subsidiaries in which they hold considerably less than 100 per cent ownership.[1] Even when local shareholders do have as

[1] An interview carried out by Franklin Weinstein with the principal representative of a major Japanese trading company in Thailand illustrates this. When asked if he did not fear that the Thais, once they had a majority of shares in the joint venture in which his company

much as 51 per cent, it is an open question whether they will show much interest in promoting policies to transfer technology to local engineers and technicians. As Vernon (1977) put it:

Almost the only area in which the interests of local shareholders and those of local government are likely to coincide is the desire to divert some of the global profits of the multinational enterprise from the rest of the network to the local subsidiary. The capacity of local stockholders to do much on that score is uncertain.

When pressured or required to offer partnership to local private investors, foreign companies may only use local people as a 'front' or 'façade'. Thus, they satisfy the letter of local aspirations while retaining effective control.

Thus, an alternative hypothesis (Hyp. 2.2) is that *Even majority partnership in overseas subsidiaries of MNCs does not necessarily confer control over policies and operations or technology transfer.* The danger of having those arrangements may be diminished when the local joint venture is a government-owned enterprise rather than a private shareholder. But it depends very much on government objectives. If control is granted simply over those aspects of the operations of MNCs which are likely to affect the economic growth of the country, or to ensure non-violation of local legislation and industrial policy, a minority partnership might be effective. Penrose (1976) suggests that a government partnership of 5 or 10 per cent can be a satisfactory means of obtaining access to information and a voice in the deliberations of the board and management.[2]

On the other hand, if the government's objective is to change the strategies and activity of a local branch of an MNC, even a 51 per cent ownership might not be sufficient. Many researchers have found that MNCs tend to adopt centralized business strategies at the

was involved, might undertake policies considered unwise by the Japanese, the executive replied: 'The joint ventures are so dependent on Japanese assistance in procuring raw material, equipment, spare parts, financing and marketing services that the local owners would be able to disregard Japanese advice only if they were prepared to sabotage the entire venture.'

[2] In the case of the Chilean government's aquisition of 51 per cent of Kennecot Copper Corporation's subsidiary, Alejandro (1970, p. 346) argued it had had beneficial side effects. 'Chileanization' of copper mines had led to large expansion plans, after many years of stagnant output. Moreover, by buying a place on the board of directors of vertically integrated activities, government gained access to valuable cost-accounting information. By training not only its own cost accountants, but also its own cadre of copper technicians and engineers, Chilean bargaining power increased *vis-à-vis* the foreign companies. Threats by foreign investors to leave could be met with less trepidation. Tax disputes could be handled with richer data. The logistics and mysteries of international merchandising may become less overpowering.

world level in order to maximize their profits worldwide. In such circumstances they may accept local partners in their subsidiaries, but they may not be prepared to give up their international policies on innovation, production and marketing in those part-owned branches.

The assumption that local ownership will cut down the future outflow of resources from the country also remains to be demonstrated. When local buyers acquire a share of existing foreign-owned facilities at market price it could be that they only are exporting scarce capital to a foreign seller, resources that might otherwise be used within the country.[3]

Brooke and Remmers (1970) raised another aspect of the problem of future outflow. Once the local affiliate has shifted from the status of wholly owned subsidiary to that of joint venture, the parent company may be tempted to penalize the joint venture by, for example, diverting business to wholly owned subsidiaries in the group, or by overpricing inwards or underpricing outwards transfers of goods and services.[4] Solomon (1978) reached similar conclusions. As he put it:

Joint ventures may pay more for technical and managerial services in the form of royalties and other fees than do wholly owned subsidiaries. A majority-owned subsidiary will generally receive greater access to the global distribution channels of its parent corporation than a joint venture.

In wholly owned subsidiaries where there is a single shareholder who also provides managerial, organizational or technological services, the shareholder expects to capture the full value of his services in the form of profits. When he is only a part owner, however, he obtains only a part of this value in proportion to his equity in the company. Thus, he may want to charge the company for the services he provides. There are several forms of payment which may be used singly or in combination. The foreign partner may receive a percentage of

[3] The Australian government's Committee of Economic Inquiry (1965) rejected a proposal to require affiliates to issue shares locally. It argued that the law would merely feed more local funds into foreign-owned enterprises, increasing foreign control of Australian industry (Behrman (1970), p. 138).

[4] Weinstein found that the Japanese partners of joint ventures in South East Asia often held responsibility for key functions such as the importation of raw material and sale of the products in export markets. This assignment is particularly important because many Japan-based MNCs find that it is these transactions, rather than the overall profitability of the joint venture, that provide the principal reward. Because the Japanese trading companies, which are the dominant force in Japanese investment in South East Asia, are involved in such diverse activities, it is normal for these transactions to take place entirely within the parent company's empire. Thus the MNC makes a profit when it sells equipment and raw material to its joint ventures. One Japanese manager in Bangkok indicated that it is not uncommon to pay up to 5 per cent above the price that would prevail if raw materials were procured in a competitive situation.

profits, fixed amount per unit of sales, lump sums and a fixed fee for specific services or for a period of time.

In general, experienced foreign negotiators are in a better position than locals to discuss details of the services they provide. Local shareholders may not be aware in precise terms of the nature, scope and value of the services. Consequently, it is difficult to determine whether the foreign partner may have inflated his total remuneration to appropriate as much from the joint venture as when the company was wholly owned.

3 TECHNOLOGY TRANSFER, TECHNOLOGICAL SELF-RELIANCE AND COMPARATIVE ADVANTAGES

The term 'technology transfer' is used with different meanings in the current literature. Some authors[1] use it as a broad concept to describe any sale or transmission of technical knowledge, even when it is part of a 'package' of capital, managerial skills and technology, which may be utilized by its purchaser but the contents of which are not completely understood.

For others,[2] technology transfer, by definition, implies assimilation of imported technology by a recipient. Over time the recipient firm may also develop the in-house capabilities to adapt, extend and perhaps improve upon the imported technology.

Mytelka (1978) notes that the capabilities to assimilate as well as to adapt, extend and improve upon imported technology are necessary components of a strategy of technological self-reliance. Technological self-reliance does not imply the notion of autarchy and isolation. It implies a dynamic process of progressively increasing the technology receiver independence to accomplish two basic objectives. First, to maximize choice through knowledge and capability. This involves developing skills which permit appropriate choice of techniques, bargaining skills which make possible improved terms for technology imports, and research and development skills which enable the firm to fathom technology, purchase components from least-cost suppliers, develop elements of the package themselves or extend the technology in order to diversify product lines. Second, a strategy of self-reliance must seek to foster local research and development into products and processes appropriate to domestic needs, resources, income and tastes (Sagasti and Guerrero, 1974).

Self-reliance as a national industrial technology strategy has been criticized by those who support neoclassical notions of comparative advantages and free market forces in creating technology. Johnson (1975) argues that the promotion of an indigenous technology in a less-developed country (LDC) requires subsidies to local industry

[1] See, for example, Behrman and Wallender, *Transfer of Manufacturing Technology within Multinational Enterprises* (1976).
[2] See, for example, Mytelka, Lynn (1978).

and protectionism against foreign technology. Indeed, LDCs have a smaller less-established technological base and level of demand for technology than the leader countries. The successful assimilation of the imported technology, its adaptation and extension, would require an enormous investment in the provision of R & D facilities and skills which would enable firms to absorb and develop new technology. Under normal conditions national firms within LDCs are unlikely to be willing and able to undertake a strategy of self-reliance without financial support and protection against direct competition from advanced foreign technology. Johnson argues:

Governments which made this mistake ignore the fact that a subsidy to one industry is necessarily a tax on others. First because any retention on investment of resources in one industry necessarily reduces the resources available to other industry . . . Second because in the modern industrial world the output of industry is typically an input into another, so that protection of the first industry imposes a tax in the form of higher input prices on the second industry.

Johnson bases his argument on the theory of comparative advantages. This was first developed by David Ricardo in England at the beginning of the nineteenth century. He stated that each country should concentrate on the production of goods for which they have a comparative cost-advantage. Through international trade, each country would gain access to the goods they do not produce. The benefits of this international division of labour, according to Ricardo, would be spread throughout the countries involved in international trade.

Johnson's argument has a serious theoretical bias. Johnson transferred a set of analytical preconceptions that were forged in developed countries as a product of their experience, and that may have served a useful purpose there, without careful consideration of their relevance for developing economies experience. The neoclassical concept of comparative advantages used in his argument does not have a universal applicability. For example, the argument that American industry enjoys comparative advantages in the production of computers and should design and manufacture them for the whole world while letting other countries concentrate on the efficient utilization of computers, can only be defended in the 'purest' economic terms. Politically, however, it is no more appealing for other countries than the suggestion, made 150 years ago, that Britain should exploit its comparative advantages in steam engines and remain the sole manufacturer for the whole world (Jequier, 1974).

Gunnar Myrdal (1968) warns that the transference of Western

concepts and theories to analyse the economic problems of under-developed countries is a serious source of bias.

Conditions in the rich Western countries today are such that, broadly speaking, the social matrix is permissive of economic development or, when not, becomes readily readjusted so as not to be placed much in the way of obstacles in its path. This is why an analysis in 'economic' terms, abstracting from the social matrix, can produce valid and useful results. But that judgement can not be accurately applied to underdeveloped countries conditions. Not only is the social and institutional structure different from the one that was involved in Western countries, but more important, the problem of development is one calling for inducing changes in that social and institutional structure, as it hinders economic development and as it does not change spontaneously, or, to any very large extent in response to policies restricted to the economic sphere.

Most modern authors of development studies[3] maintain that a major cause of underdevelopment is precisely the way underdeveloped countries are placed in the international division of labour. A major argument is that international trade increasingly benefits the producers of industrial goods and penalizes primary goods producers.

In the second half of the twentieth century, many underdeveloped countries, and especially the so-called 'NICs', have become industrialized. But they are still dependent upon developed countries for financial and technological resources. The international division of labour has now shifted to producers and non-producers of technology assets.

An international division of labour in science and technology which leaves large areas without any independent scientific capacity is unacceptable to countries which are aiming to develop an independent industrial base. As Freeman (1974) stated:

Simply to assimilate any sophisticated technology today, and operate it efficiently, requires some independent capacity for R and D, even if this is mainly adaptive R and D.

There are also economic reasons for developing countries to undertake R & D activities. The learning-by-doing process is, by itself, a source of external economies. Learning-by-doing, according to Arrow (1962), is to seize every opportunity to solve problems associated with the choice of technique, technology suppliers, machinery and of the very products to produce, in order to develop the in-house capability to assimilate imported technology.

Cooper and Maxwell (1975) argued that private enterprises in developing countries have to decide whether to purchase foreign

[3] See, for example, Sunkel, O. and Paz, P.; Santos, T. (1969); Salama, P. (1976); Furtado, C.

skills (which are proven commercially) or to run the risks and meet the costs of building local ones.

But enterprises may not benefit from the skills that would be developed if they were to use say local economists and engineers for feasibility studies, or local engineering constructors, or a local variant of the process technology, rather than foreign counterparts. The skills that are built up may be more beneficial to other firms; they are external to the firm itself. So, the individual private enterprise left to itself in the world technology market will attach less importance to building up local technological skills than the society as a whole . . . Consequently, from a communal point of view, the hegemony of static comparative advantage in technical capabilities is unacceptable and the state must interfere in the market to produce socially optimal results.

Another argument against the neoclassical idea of leaving it to market forces to determine the international creation and commercialization of technical knowledge is the reality of existing imperfect markets for technology. For Schumpeter (1939), a successful innovation allows a firm to capture 'super-normal' profits temporarily before its competitors are able to imitate the innovation. Cooper and Maxwell noted two implications of this for the technology-transfer process.

The first is that the technology has economic value to the innovator. If he were to allow free use of this technology, the period of quasi-monopoly would be shorter than if he kept it to himself—so there would be less super-normal profit. Consequently, the innovator will not allow other firms to use his technology unless he is assured of getting a return which is commensurate with what he would have got had he expanded his own production—hence licensing fees, royalties and the like. Often, the innovator (or technology supplier) will seek a substantial measure of control over the use of his technology, in order to ensure expected returns or to prevent the recipient enterprise from competing with him.

This control limits the learning-by-doing process and tends to perpetuate the hegemony of foreign technology or what is usually called 'technology dependence'.

The second implication 'is that the quasi-monopoly which comes from possessing the technology puts the innovator in a much stronger bargaining position than any firm which may want to license the technology'. As a result, the technology supplier is in a position to be able to impose higher prices, establish control over licensees' business strategies and impose requirements to purchase input packages which include items that could be procured under better conditions from third parties. When alternative sources are local, the importing of a package reduces the potential market for other domestic activities.

This is not due to any lack of efficiency or availability of local production as Johnson would argue, but because of the strings involved in packages enforced by the licenser.

4 LICENSING STRATEGIES AND COMPETITIVE IMPLICATIONS

The sale of technology[1] through licensing is mainly an international activity. A number of studies indicate that firms tend to license their technology internationally more readily than domestically.[2] Wilson (1975) attributes this tendency especially to the oligopoly view of owners of inventions[3] who seek to preserve the market for themselves. They may be willing, however, to license their technology to overseas firms that are not expected to be direct competitors.

This study of the Brazilian computer industry will deal mainly with technological agreements which involve the license to manufacture patented products and access to specifications and technical drawings. This may also include technical assistance to manufacture the products—identification of tools and equipment to be used, assembling techniques and quality control.

Licensing and foreign investment are both part of the process by which manufacturing firms exploit their advantages abroad (Sercovich, 1975). Some studies[4] indicate that firms' preference is for foreign operations with a package of capital, managerial skills and technical knowledge rather than simply licensing their know-how.

There are three explanations for the apparent preference for linking licensing and equity shares. The first emphasizes the role of international oligopolistic competition for market shares (Hymer, 1960). If MNCs sell their technology without linking it to investment,

[1] Technology sale or transfer is a generic term for a contract which involves transmission of technical knowledge. In Brazil, according to Law number 4131 from 27 September 1962, there are five categories of transfer:
(1) technical assistance;
(2) manufacturing license and/or patent utilization permission;
(3) license to brands and trade marks utilization;
(4) engineering service;
(5) project elaboration.
[2] See Wilson, R. (1975) and Casson, M. (1979).
[3] The term 'invention' as used by Wilson may also mean 'innovation'. According to Schumpeter an 'invention' is an idea, a sketch or a model for a new improved device, product or system. Such inventions may be patented but they do not necessarily lead to technical innovations. An innovation in the economic sense is accomplished only with the first commercial transaction involving the new product, process, system or device.
[4] See Johnson, H., *Technology and Economic Interdependence*, Macmillan, 1975.

they might be strengthening a competitor's position in the market by supplying a resource which they presently lack. The second explanation is that foreign direct investment is associated with oligopolistic product differentiation (Caves, 1971). The successful transfer of sophisticated and non-homogeneous products often requires a continuing relationship between the supplier and the receiver, such as provided by an international firm structure. Consequently, the rent the firm can obtain abroad for its knowledge must be tied to the process of production and distribution. A third explanation is concerned with the sale of intermediate goods when technology has reached a mature stage. As Terumo Ozawa (1971) said:

Being unable to expect profits from the sale of standardized technology, transferors try to compensate for the bargain sale of technology by securing or monopolizing the supply of intermediate goods such as raw materials, parts and components. To this end, capital ownership and management participation become strategically important.

It has been argued, however, that evolutionary trends in the world economy have changed corporate viewpoints about foreign involvements and management of their technological assets (Baranson, 1978). Consequently, a growing number of corporations are adopting an explicit policy of shifting from equity investment and managerial control of overseas facilities to the direct sale of technology and management services as a means of earning returns on corporate assets. There are five major factors that have influenced trends in these directions:

(i) the demand of newly industrialized countries for technology sharing;
(ii) the intensified political risks and economic uncertainties of overseas capital investments in plants and equipment;
(iii) the shifting emphasis in certain firms from production to R & D functions (investment in technology may provide higher rates of return than investment in expansion of production capacity);
(iv) the intensified competition from foreign enterprises as suppliers of industrial technology and the resulting pressure to release proprietary technology early in the product's life;
(v) the increasing costs of direct investment abroad.

Most of these factors are related to constraints on foreign investment. These involve host-government restrictions on trade and direct investment and the fact that some licensers may be relatively small and thus not have sufficient financial and managerial resources to invest abroad.[5] Thus they choose pure licensing agreements.

One example of the role of size in technology trends is provided by small electronics firms whose competitive strengths are based on product design rather than manufacturing knowledge or financial strength. Since they do not have the necessary resources to manufacture abroad or to export on a large scale, those firms usually prefer to sell the designs. On the other hand, large electronics firms which possess manufacturing and technological know-how as well as financial resources usually adopt business strategies abroad that involve the application of a combination of those resources.

Sercovich (1975) emphasized the size constraint argument by comparing US and UK foreign fees and royalty earnings from affiliated and non-affiliated firms. The findings were that in the 1960s, in the USA, foreign royalties paid by non-affiliated firms accounted for only 24 per cent of the royalties. The figure for the UK was 70 per cent. He explained:

With the exception of a few large multinational companies (ICI, Unilever) UK firms operating abroad may reply on pure licensing operations in order to penetrate foreign markets because of their relatively weaker competitive standing.

Therefore, there are alternative hypotheses concerning firms' strategy in exploiting their technology abroad to be examined in this study of the Brazilian computer industry. (Hyp. 3.1) is that *Licenser firms prefer to offer a 'package' of equity investment, managerial skills and technical knowledge rather than just license their know-how.* Alternatively, (Hyp. 3.2) is that *In recent years, licensers have shifted their preference from equity investment and management control to the sale of technology and management services.*

For subsidiaries of multinational firms, the licensing link is part of a broader intracompany relationship. But in the case of independent firms there is, at least in theory, a choice between acquiring the technology abroad or developing it in-house.

[5] Technology import through pure licensing is, in general, welcomed by national governments. In 1965 a report from the French Minister of Industry stated that 'it was acceptable to buy foreign technology when it assisted national enterprises in making a major innovation profitable or supported a new process of production developed by French industry—being complementary to a national initiative. Minor innovation could be accepted from abroad, as has been done in several sectors with frequent exchange techniques and which are of a nature such as to stimulate or complement national efforts. Neither of these two last types of technology imports were considered threatening to the economy and therefore did not warrant imposition of protectionist measures.'

There are four basic explanations for such firms deciding to acquire technology through licensing agreements instead of developing it autonomously. The first is related to the complexity of technology. Firms enter into licensing agreements to obtain access to product or process designs which they could not develop in-house. They may be firms with previous experience in the market, but without the technical capabilities or the necessary R & D structure to produce the required new design, or firms entering a new market; or when the amount of technological change required exceeds in-house capacity to generate new products.

This study will explore the reasons for undertaking licensing agreements in the Brazilian computer industry. (Hyp. 4.1) is that *Licensing is made necessary by the complexity of technology.*

A second explanation relates licensing to the competitive environment. In LDCs locally owned firms may have the necessary skill to design and develop their own product line. But products designed locally may not be competitive with foreign competitive products. When at least one firm operating within a particular LDC market introduces innovations developed abroad, firms with the technological strategy of self-reliance are challenged. The innovation may be introduced either by a subsidiary of an MNC which adopts a world-wide product policy or by a locally owned firm with licensing links with a foreign firm. The consequence is that the pattern of product competition in the LDC's market becomes similar to that existing in the international market. Thus local firms are unlikely to adapt themselves to the new level of product competition without relying on a foreign company as well.[6]

Therefore, (Hyp. 4.2) is that *Licensing is made necessary by the competitive environment.*

A third reason for undertaking licensing agreements is related to cost advantages and to the risks of undertaking product development in-house. Licensing agreements may be a cheaper alternative to designing and developing products and processes in-house. This may be particularly important for firms willing to manufacture a mature product in an advanced phase of its life cycle. Also, product development involves risks which can be avoided by using foreign technology which has already been proven commercially. The next hypothesis (Hyp. 4.3) is that *Licensing is made necessary by the cost advantage and risks of own product development.*

A fourth explanation for the decision to acquire technology

---

[6] In his study of 123 Argentinian firms, Sercovich (1975) found that the major reason for licensing was that it permitted national firms to enter oligopolistic markets in which competition was structured by the standards set through foreign imports.

through licensing is the goodwill enjoyed by some foreign brand names in the local market and previous relationships with the licensers. Mytelka (1978) studied the reasons for undertaking licensing agreements by metalworking and chemical firms located in Peru, Ecuador and Colombia. More than half of the firms interviewed gave 'brand-name' considerations as one of the reasons for licensing, thus implying entry into a 'quality segment' of the market in which standards had been set by foreign imports.

A typical situation which leads to licensing agreements is when a marketing subsidiary or an independent distributor faces tariff protection and import restrictions. The simplest way to overcome these barriers is to start up local manufacturing activities to substitute for imports. In so far as local production is encouraged by a previously existing demand, the firm should manufacture products as similar as possible to the imported ones. This requires importing product and process designs. Hypothesis (Hyp. 4.4) is that *Licensing is made necessary by the advantages of gaining access to particular brand names and by previous relationship with licensers.*

Licensing is related to the technological strategy pursued by the firm. In determining strategy any firm confronts a range of technological and market constraints. It can use its technical skills in different ways. Freeman (1974) classifies six technological strategies of manufacturing firms. Firms may recognizably follow one or another of these strategies and they may change from one strategy to another or follow different strategies in different sectors of their business. Of Freeman's six types of strategies, the four relevant to the present work are described briefly.

A *dependent strategy* is pursued by firms which play an essentially satellite or subordinate role in relation to another firm. The dependent firm makes no effort to initiate or to imitate technical changes in its product line, except as a result of specific requests from its customers or its parents (if it is a subsidiary). They usually rely on licensing agreements and have no R & D facilities. The dependent firm may retain a limited degree of autonomy. In this situation the only developmental capability needed is the ability to evaluate and select foreign technology. This involves project evaluation, industrial engineering and management skills.

An *imitative strategy* consists in following way behind the leaders in established technologies. The main difference between dependent and imitative strategy is that the latter involves a conscious effort to adapt foreign technology after acquiring it. The extent of the lag between an imitative firm and a leader firm will vary depending upon the particular circumstances of the industry, the country and the firm. Imitative firms usually rely on licensing, but have some in-house capabilities in adaptive development and product and process engineering.

The imitator must enjoy certain advantages to enter the market in competition with the established innovating firms. These may include a 'captive market' (e.g. another associated firm) or decisive cost advantages (e.g. lower labour costs, plant investment costs, energy supplies, transport costs or material costs). Imitative firms' advantages may be due to government protection such as 'market reserve' and tariff protection. The enterprising imitator may aspire to become a 'defensive' innovator, especially in rapidly growing economies.

A *defensive strategy* is usually pursued by firms which want to avoid the risks of being the first to introduce a new product. Firms adopting defensive strategies may hope to take advantage of the original innovator's mistakes and improve upon their design, manu-facturing and marketing. Attempts are made to follow the leading industrial firms as closely as possible. They must have a strong R & D capability, but may lack the capacity or the willingness for the more original types of innovation, and in particular the links with fundamental research. Alternatively, they may have particular strengths and skills in marketing and production engineering. Such firms are typical in oligopolistic markets and differentiate their products by technical improvements. They try to compete by developing an independent patent position rather than simply by taking a licence, but they may undertake licensing agreements as a spring-board to improve on the product.

In general the large multiproduct firm in technology-intensive industries contain elements of both 'defensive' and 'offensive' strategies in their various product lines. Defensive strategies are characteristics of firms in the smaller industrialized countries, which lack the scientific environment and the market to stimulate offensive technological strategies.

An *offensive innovation strategy* aims to achieve technical and market leadership in the introduction of new products and processes. Offensive firms are research intensive and rely heavily upon in-house R & D. They must have a very strong problem-solving capacity in designing, building and testing prototypes. Only a small minority of firms in any country are willing to follow an offensive strategy over a long period.

Dependent and imitative strategies are pursued by almost all firms in developing countries. Multinationals' subsidiaries generally have a technologically dependent role, although they vary in the way they are organized and in the degree of autonomy they are allowed by their parents. Defensive and offensive strategies are found essentially in developed countries.

Freeman (1974) believes that a developing country economy may adopt an industrial structure which relies on dependent strategies. He argues:

> But if it does so it is likely to remain extremely poor and backward. Even a successful imitative strategy, although it may lead to industrial development, will reach a point when export competitiveness in labour costs may increasingly conflict with the goal of higher per capita income.

It is possible for an individual firm, or for a country's industrial system as a whole, to change technological strategies. The necessary condition to change from dependent to imitative and defensive strategies is the acquisition and development of skills such as adaptive development, production engineering, product and process design and management. Also important is the size of the market, local availability of scientific and technological inputs, technical capacity of local engineers and managers and appropriate government policies. Japan is an example of successful change in technological strategy. In less than thirty years, some Japanese industries such as consumer electronics and petrochemicals have moved from an imitative to a defensive and finally to an offensive innovation strategy.

Technology evolution is not achieved without commitment of firms. Firms must aim to acquire innovative capabilities as a means to long-term profits. This may occur in firms where local management has the autonomy to change their technological strategies. When a firm is an MNC subsidiary, typically the final authority to choose technical strategies rests with the parent. Often the subsidiary receives only part of a total production process, for example the final assembly or the production of some components. In general it does not take part in product and process design and its responsibility is restricted to the operational level. Even some minor adaptation in product design, for example, to allow the use of local inputs, tend to be undertaken in the R & D laboratory of the parent firm. Under these conditions the subsidiary's dependency is an explicit strategy within the strategy of the corporation as a whole.

Locally owned firms may sometimes be also unwilling and unable to move away from a dependent technological strategy. This may occur when firms are operating under licensing agreements. Erber (1974) found that Brazilian firms manufacturing capital goods under licence rarely made a real effort to understand the product design. Constraints on licensees' learning processes may also stem from the supply side. Licensers may retain control over important logistic and strategic decisions within the licensed firm and 'impose' a dependent strategy upon it.

Because of the acceptance of the licensed products in the local market, licensees adopting a dependent strategy may enjoy good profits for considerable periods. Local shareholders may succeed in retaining formal ownership independence, but they are usually under the risk of having the licence withdrawn or being taken over by technology suppliers.

5   LICENSING AND CONTROL

The distinction between ownership and control of firms was already observed as early as 1920. The *'Reichsfinanzhof'* of Germany developed the *'Organtheorie'*, stating that a company is in a position of organic subordination when, in spite of legal autonomy, it is economically, financially or organizationally controlled by another firm (Sercovich, 1975).

Organizational dependence was claimed to occur when the same people sit on the Board of Directors of each company. Financial subordination arises when another firm controls more than 50 per cent of equity shares. Economic subordination arises when another enterprise commands decisions concerning pricing, methods of processing raw materials, components and equipment purchase.

With foreign investment, these three types of control may exist. With pure-licensing agreements, however, control may only be exercised through economic subordination.

One firm can control another directly or through the market control. Market control can be exercised by cartel arrangements amongst technology suppliers, and by patent or other institutional protection. Direct control can be exercised by control over *basic decisions* and over *logistic and strategic decisions.*

Control over *basic decisions* concerns decisions about capital raising and expenditure, dividend policy and organizational policy. Technology recipients without equity links with licensers may maintain their decision-making capacity with regard to basic decisions.

Control of logistic and strategic decisions appears to be the most important area for control. This includes four major functions:

1   MARKETING FUNCTIONS

This involves control over markets, prices, advertising and promotion methods, marketing strategies, distribution systems and packaging and labelling specifications.

The most common type of control over marketing functions is

export restrictions. This can assume many forms. Licensing agreements may include clauses involving a total ban on exports, export prohibitions to specific countries, a requirement for prior approval of exports, quotas, price control, permission for export to specific firms only and restrictions on the use of trade marks in exports.

The purpose of clauses prohibiting exports embodying the imported technology is to restrict competition among licensees. But it can deprive the local firm of marketing incentives which might induce innovation.

Vaitsos (1971) studied restrictive clauses on exports in licensing agreements held in four Latin American countries (Bolivia, Peru, Columbia and Ecuador). He found that about 81 per cent of the contracts totally prohibited exports and 86 per cent had some restrictive clause on exports. Vaitsos explained that

. . . restrictive clauses on exports are set on the basis of relative bargaining power given conditions on alternative sources of supply of technology. Thus, countries such as those in the Andean Pact despite the diverging size and relative strength of their firms do not achieve major concessions in terms of their negotiations with foreign transnational corporations that sell industrial technology.

In Brazil the government bodies in charge of the approval of licensing agreements (Banco Central and INPI) refuse registration of contracts with export restriction clauses. This may appear to be counter to the interests of licensers, but one study reported that this does not represent an important constraint in the conclusion of new licensing agreements (Erber, 1974). Verbal and 'gentlemen's' agreements may substitute for explicit export restriction clauses.

Another form of control over marketing activities is the offering of exclusive marketing rights. This grants the foreign partner the exclusive right to purchase all or part of the output of the company for export. Such arrangements are common when the foreign company has facilities for further processing, and the local company is essentially a source of materials or cheap labour force.

Exclusive marketing rights may improve exports but involves the danger that the local company obtains only a low return because of the monopsonistic position of the foreign firm.

2 PRODUCT STRATEGY

Product strategy includes product selection, design, production, testing and planning. Control in licensing agreements is generally exercised through restrictive clauses. These can assume the following forms:

— Quality control by the licenser.
— Prohibition of introduction of modifications or improvements without the licenser's authorization in advance.
— Prohibition of the use of licensed knowledge after the end of the agreement.
— Obligation to grant back to the licenser a royalty-free, world-wide license on any improvement or modification in licensed products.
— Prohibition of the production of competitive products, utilization of alternative processes or exploitation of alternative trademarks to those licensed.

Technology suppliers may exercise control over licensees' product policy in order to ensure the quality of final output. But this limits the extent of recipients' decision-making capability and reduces capacity to absorb and develop the licensed technology through learning-by-doing. By limiting licensees' autonomy in modifying product design, licensers ensure mechanical aspects, standardized componentry and compatibility with existing peripherals in computer products.

Clauses requiring the transfer to the supplier of innovations or improvements obtained through the use of imported technology may remove the financial incentive to research and develop new products.

3   PRODUCTION AND TECHNICAL FUNCTIONS

Production and technical functions involve two major activities: selection of process techniques and selection of equipment.

When the subject of the licensing agreement is process technology, the mechanisms of control may be the same as for product technology. However, when licensing refers to product design, the control may derive mainly from technical assistance given by the licenser. Some explicit conditions may also be included in the agreement, for example, the reservation of the right to decide what modifications may be introduced concerning the technique to manufacture licensed products.

In general, technology embodied in a particular plant is not interchangeable with similar technology supplied by other producers. Spare parts and machinery from a different source may not be compatible with existing machinery. Consequently, replacement of existing capacity must usually be carried out through the original supplier thus tying the recipient. Under these circumstances the initial choice of a particular form of technology may at times also determine the source of supply for a large variety of items connected with the technology in use (Penrose, 1976).

Ownership links are related to dependence upon production and technical functions. Mytelka (1978) found that 93 per cent of the subsidiaries of MNCs in Andean countries obtained their technology either directly from their parent or licenser or from a firm recommended by them.

Suppliers may want to control production and technical decisions in order to ensure the efficiency of the plant, as returns depend to some extent on the performance of the plant. However, this kind of control may seriously constrain local firms' technological strategies.

4   PROCUREMENT POLICY

Procurement policy involves the selection of sources of supply of raw materials, component parts and other inputs. The dangers of procurement policy dependence are that it may limit the learning-by-doing and that it is associated with monopoly pricing of tied inputs. Also it may restrain competition among sources of supply.

The major form of licensers' influence in licensees' procurement policies is tie-in clauses on intermediate products.[1] These clauses require purchase of intermediate goods from the same source of that for know-how. In three Andean countries (Bolivia, Peru and Ecuador), explicit requirements for the purchase of material from the technology supplier were found in 67 per cent of all contracts for technology commercialization (Vaitsos, 1971).

The nature of know-how sold could, however, predetermine the source of intermediate products, even in the absence of explicit terms. The present work will assess the nature and extent of licensers' control over logistic and strategic decisions (marketing functions, product strategy, production and technical functions and procurement policy) in the Brazilian computer industry.

---

[1] Tie-in clauses, especially those attached to patents which go beyond the scope of the patent, are illegal under the anti-trust laws of the USA, the Restrictive Practices Act of the UK and the European Community under the Treaty of Rome (Penrose, 1976).

PART TWO

6 THE BRAZILIAN COMPUTER INDUSTRY

1 DEFINITIONS

The computer industry is really a closely-linked network of industry and commercial activities, encompassing both manufacturing and service activities, centering on the production, and utilization of goods and services based on computers and related technologies, in both their hardware and software aspects.

(Canada, SC, 1973.)

Figure 6.1 shows the range of computer hardware products which are presently manufactured by the international computer industry.

(a) Computers

Differentiation between size of computers is usually based on memory capacity, bits per word, input/output speed, price, range of peripherals, etc. Because of the rapidly changing technology, clear differentiation based on size of computers quickly became out of date. Table 6.1 shows the basic characteristics recently introduced to differentiate computers.

(b) Peripherals

Peripheral devices link the computer with the external world, and include input/output through terminals, card readers, printers and a variety of other devices. Peripheral equipment is also used for auxiliary storage. In most computer systems peripherals account for a major share of the overall cost.

(b.1) Terminals

Terminals have input and output capabilities and provide a means of communication with the computer in an interactive or conversational manner. There are several types of terminals being manufactured in Brazil. These include bank terminals, video display units (VDUs), data-entry equipment and point-of-sale terminals (POS).

Bank terminals are designed to automate transactions with bank customers. Examples of these terminals are automatic telling

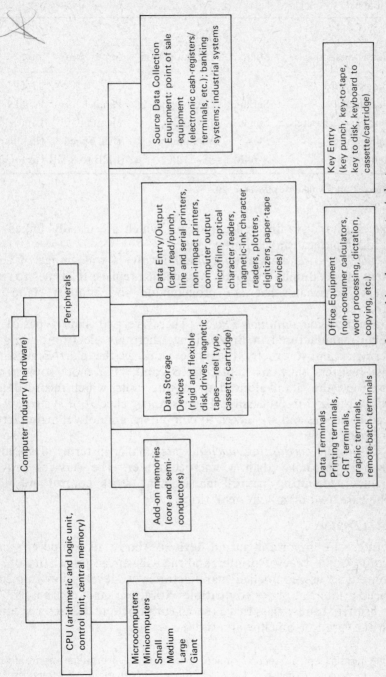

Fig. 6.1 Range of products manufactured by the computer industry.

Table 6.1.

| Characteristics | Micro | Mini | | Maxi |
		Common Mini	Super Mini	
Bits per word	8	16	22	32–64
Processing	Serial	Overlapping	Parallel	Parallel
Number of channels	Single	Limited	Medium	Large
Input/output	Slow	Medium	High Speed	High Speed
Memory	8–64K	48–512K	1 MB to 8 MB	Up to 32 MB

Source: Carlos Valdesuso (1981), p. 20.

machines and on-line teller systems, which are usually linked to a minicomputer installed in the bank.

VDUs and data-entry equipment involve a wide range of equipment from 'dumb' terminals intended to replace teletypes to 'intelligent' terminals that are programable and support stand-alone processing.

Point-of-sale terminals (POS). There are two main types of POS being manufactured in Brazil. First, there are electronic units that perform almost exactly the same work as the electro-mechanical cash-registers they are replacing. Second, at a more sophisticated level, are the 'stand-alone data capture units' which record data on floppy disks for processing. Laser scanner check-out systems which read bar-codes and are linked to computers, are not yet manufactured in Brazil.

Electronic accounting machines are smaller in terms of speed and memory capacity than a microcomputer. The services provided include accounting, payroll management, stock control and billing. They are used mainly in small firms.

(b.2) *Printers*

Printers are important output devices. Almost all computer systems require some type of printer, and the widespread popularity of small computers has compelled manufacturers to develop low-to-medium speed printers at prices compatible with those small computers.

Printers can be classified as serial (printing one character at a time) or line (printing one line at a time).

Line printers are, in general, much faster than serial printers but are also considerably more expensive. However, the price/cost of line printers, especially slower ones, is falling, primarily because of their increased use on small computers.

(Lines, 1980.)

(b.3) *Magnetic storage devices*

There are four main types of magnetic storage devices: tape drives, cassette recorders, disk drives and floppy-disk drives.

Tape memories or drives are used for large bulk storage of computer data, without which the computer would be limited to extremely small computations.

Cassette recorders are low-cost systems intended to replace punched paper tape. The advantage of cassette over paper include ease of handling, less operation intervention, better editing capabilities, and higher reliability.   (Lines, 1980.)

Magnetic-disk drives store a smaller quantity of data than tape drives, but they deliver data more rapidly to the computer. The market for disk drives is growing fast because of the cost and speed advantages of these direct-access storage devices for many kinds of computer applications. *Floppy-disk drives* represent the low-end segment of the disk systems market due to their lower performance and price. Floppy disks are used mainly in mini and microcomputers. The new Winchester technology is enabling a substantial increase in disk-storage capacity.

(b.4) *Modems*

Modems are utilized to *mod*ulate and *demod*ulate computer data for communication purposes. The demand is growing fast due to the increasing importance of computer networks and distributed data processing.

(c) Software

Software is a set of programs or routines concerned with the operation of a computer system. Software may be divided in two broad categories: system software and application software. System software serves two major purposes: it aids the development of both system and application software and it controls the execution of software on the computer. Applications software is the program or set of programs that performs the functions specified by the end user. It essentially makes the hardware and system software transparent to the user and is considered the highest level of software.   (Lines, 1980.)

2 SIZE

In 1981 Brazil's total market for computing equipment reached US $1 billion (see Table 6.2).

Until 1975 Brazil depended almost entirely on imports to satisfy its growing needs for computing equipment, since domestic production was still at an early stage of development. In that year severe import restrictions were introduced by Capre, the government body in charge of computer policy at this time, and a fixed annual quota was established for imports of computers and related products,

Table 6.2 Estimate of the Brazilian market for computers and peripherals, 1981

Item	US$ million
Locally manufactured, of which:	1147
Brazilian firms	416.6
MNCs' subsidiaries	730.4
Imports (final products)	105[a]
Exports (final products)	244
Local market	1008

[a] Includes computers imported as capital investment, without foreign currency expenditure.

including components for local assembly. In 1981 the quota was fixed at a level of US $200 million: $125 million (62.5 per cent) for components; $20 million (10 per cent) for spare parts for existing systems; and $55 million (27.5 per cent) for final products. Total imports grew at a geometric rate of 27.9 per cent a year between 1969 and 1981 (see Figure 6.2).

Widespread introduction of information-processing systems in many sectors of the Brazilian economy fuelled the rapid increase in sales of computers. In 1980 the total computer population reached 8844 units from 1219 in 1974. Micro and minicomputers showed the highest growth rates. In 1980 they represented 72 per cent of the total computer population compared with only 38 per cent in 1972 (see Table 6.3 and Figure 6.3).

Comparing data for various countries, Table 6.4 shows the 1980 and 1981 estimates of the market for computers in the USA, Japan and Western European countries. Brazil ranks, in absolute terms,

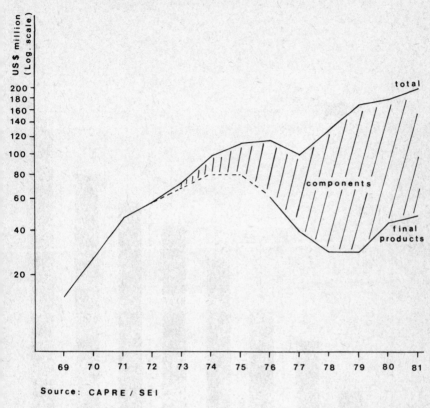

Fig. 6.2 Brazilian imports of DP equipment and components (1969-81)

Table 6.3 Computers installed in Brazil, 1980

Class of computer	Quantity	Per cent of total
Micro	4722	53.4
Mini	1675	18.9
Small	1688	19.0
Medium	388	4.4
Large	248	2.8
Very large	123	1.4
Total	8844	100.0

Source: Secretaria Especial de Informatica.

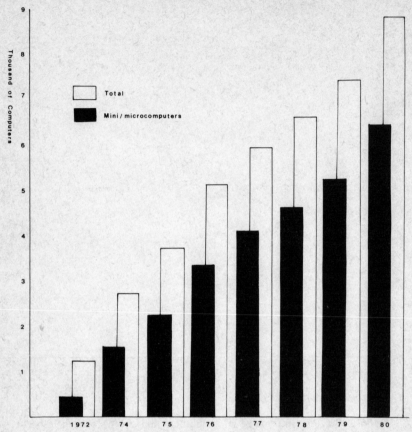

Fig. 6.3 Computers installed in Brazil (1972–80)

between seventh and eleventh in the world computer market.[1] The Brazilian market equals about one-fifth of the German, one-quarter of the British and French and more than half the Italian market for computer products. However, the sale of computer products in Brazil is growing faster than in these countries.

In Brazil minicomputers have been increasingly utilized in business management applications in small- and medium-size firms. In a survey on minicomputer customers it was found that 60 per cent of the firms spent between 1.5 and 2.0 per cent of total turnover on computer operations. It can be assumed, therefore, that the

[1] The exact position of Brazil in the world computer ranking could not be estimated here because recent data on the computer market in the USSR, Canada and Australia were not available. Also, data for Scandinavia and Benelux shown in Table 6.4 are not broken down for individual countries.

Table 6.4 Estimate of the computer and related equipment market in various countries 1980 and 1981

Country	Market value—US $ million		
	1980	1981	% growth
United States	30 733.8	35 951.6	16.9
Japan	8355.9	9408.9	12.6
Western Europe (total)	17 090.9	19 212.4	12.4
West Germany	4607.3	5064.2	9.9
France	3523.7	4033.9	14.5
United Kingdom	3524.0	4025.8	14.2
Italy	1673.6	1924.0	15.0
Benelux	1308.9	1428.8	9.2
Scandinavia	958.7	1080.0	12.7
Spain	824.4	916.6	11.2
Switzerland	406.8	449.1	10.4
Brazil	755.6	1008.0	33.4

Source: *Electronics International*, 13 January 1981.

Note: The statistics for Western Europe were originally aggregated. The numbers for individual countries were estimated based on an average percentage of computer products in total electronic equipment markets of those countries.

'typical' minicomputer user is a firm with total annual sales ranging from US $500 000 to US $1 000 000. Minicomputers have also been used as intelligent terminals in larger systems, and in data communication applications. Another major user is the banking sector, where minicomputer systems are utilized as stand-alone machines and as preprocessors, data-input devices, and intelligent terminals.

The public sector, including state and municipal government and public enterprise, account for 45.6 per cent of the Brazilian market for computers and services. However, the state uses mainly medium, large and very large computers. Consequently, its relative importance as a customer for the national minicomputer manufacturers is lower than the extent that its market share may suggest. Table 6.5 shows state participation by sector in total expenditure on data-processing activities in Brazil.

The market for minicomputers used for scientific and process control applications is still limited. Operations such as process control make intensive use of skilled and semi-skilled labour. This is still cheap in Brazil and the substitution of sophisticated computers

Table 6.5 Public sector expenditure on data-processing activities as a percentage of Brazilian total, 1980

Sector	Per cent of total market
Federal government, of which:	32.20
Finance	16.94
Mining and energy	3.47
Social services	2.33
Communications	1.62
Planning	1.57
Transport	1.29
Education	1.21
Others	3.57
State and municipal governments	13.40
Total	45.6

Source: *Dados e Ideias*, vol. 7, no. 3, August 1981, p. 9.

for this inexpensive factor of production is not seen as economically justified. Figure 6.4 shows the distribution of computers installed in Brazil by sector of activities.

3   INDUSTRY STRUCTURE

In Brazil, in 1980, computer hardware manufacturers, including subsidiaries of MNCs, employed about 15 000 people, and sales, both internal and exports, are estimated at more than US $1100 million. Figure 6.5 shows the value of the trade between hardware, software, and components suppliers in Brazil and overseas.

A comprehensive chart of the Brazilian computer industry is presented in Figure 6.6. It includes all hardware manufacturers in Brazil and their equity, technology, and marketing links within the country and abroad. Figure 6.6 also shows the world-wide technology and financial links between foreign firms which have links with the Brazilian computer industry.

(a) Medium and large computer systems

In 1980 there was about 2500 mainframe computers installed in Brazil. Most suppliers were engaged in the business of marketing and servicing mainframes and peripherals imported from the USA.

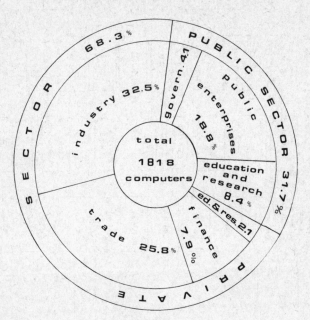

Fig. 6.4 Distribution of installed computers according to sector of activities (1976). Excludes minicomputers

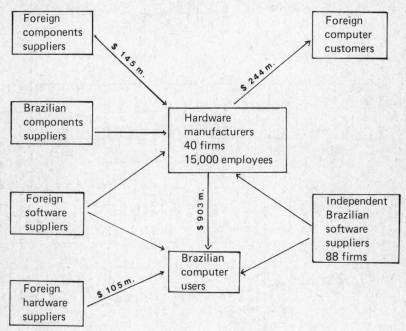

Fig. 6.5 The Brazilian computer industry, 1980

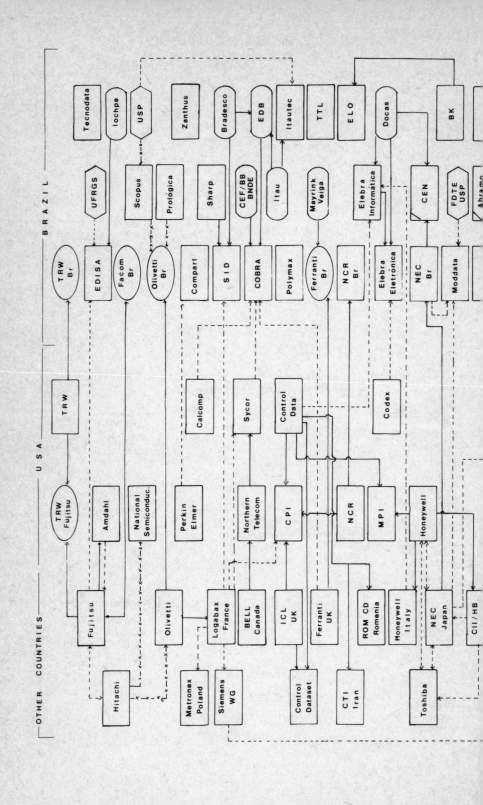

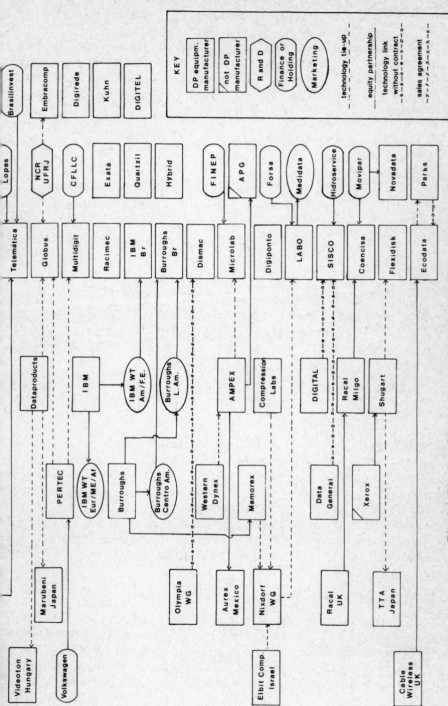

Fig. 6.6 The Brazilian computer industry and its links worldwide

The exceptions were IBM, Burroughs and CII-Honeywell Bull (in a joint venture with local groups), which assemble computers locally. Table 6.6 shows the number of computers installed in Brazil in July 1980 by manufacturer and the type of equipment manufactured locally.

Table 6.6 Medium to large computers installed in Brazil and type of equipment manufactured locally

| | | Computer installed in Brazil | | |
Firm	Medium to large equipment manufactured in Brazil (1981)	Small and medium	Large and very Large	Total
IBM	4331 (1 to 2 MB) 4341 (2 to 8 MB)	902	295	1197
Hewlett-Packard		328	–	328
Burroughs	B–6900 (2.3 to 6.2 MB)	283	38	321
Digital	–	251	–	251
CII-Honeywell Bull	Telematic 1, 2, 3 (from 2 MB)	115	19	134
Univac	–	84	11	95
Facom (Fujitsu)	–	47	3	50
Others	–	66	5	71
Total		2076	371	2447

Source: SEI.

Figure 6.7 shows the evolution of market shares in the Brazilian computer population from July 1975 to July 1980. The apparent decline of IBM is deceptive. While HP is growing fast in medium and small computers, IBM retains its position in large systems with much higher unit prices. In 1980 IBM's share of the Brazilian market was estimated to be more than 60 per cent in terms of the value of the installed equipment. The distribution of installed computers per manufacturer in 1980 is shown in Figure 6.8.

(b) Micro and minicomputers

In Brazil there are five major minicomputer manufacturers. They are Cobra, Edisa, Labo, SID and Sisco. There are some other microcomputer manufacturers which operate in the low-end segment of the computer system market. Hewlett-Packard is the only foreign firm with local manufacturing activities in microcomputer systems. But it only produces a scientific microcomputer model. All other manufacturers are locally owned since this segment of the market

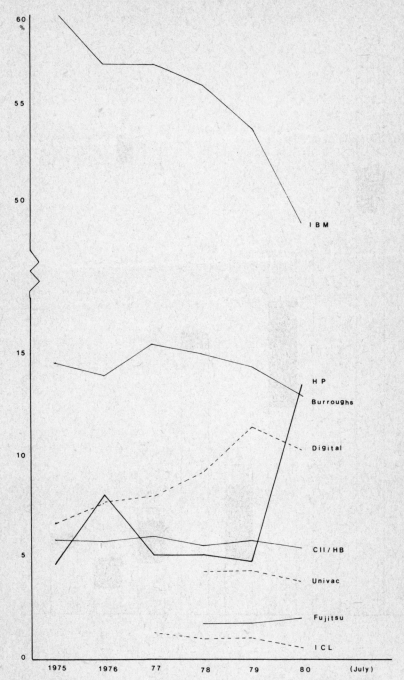

Fig. 6.7 Percentage of computers installed in Brazil per manufacturer

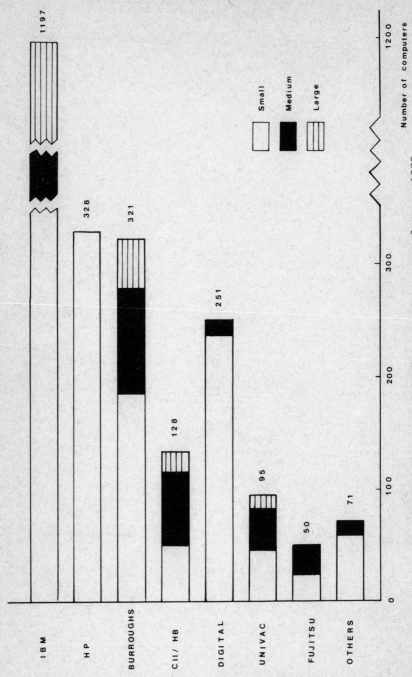

Fig. 6.8 Distribution of installed computers per manufacturers, 1980

is under the 'market reserve policy', a policy designed to save micro and minicomputer manufacturing for locally owned firms.

The manufacture of mini computers in Brazil began in 1978 on a large scale. In that year Olivetti and Burroughs were the major suppliers of imported equipment, accounting for 77.5 per cent of minicomputers installed (see Figure 6.9). Since then there has been an increasing substitution of locally manufactured minicomputers for imported ones. In 1980 local firms accounted for 22 per cent of all mini and microcomputer systems installed. This percentage is expected to double in 1982.

Government sources estimate that in 1981 sales of minicomputers will reach about 1500 units (see Table 6.7).

Table 6.7 Estimate of minicomputer sales in Brazil, 1981–4

| Year | Number of systems | |
	Capre/SEI	Digibras
1981	1684	1488
1982	2022	1785
1983	2426	2142
1984	2911	2571

Abicomp, the Brazilian Computer Manufacturers' Association, estimates that in 1981 the computer market will absorb 1800 minicomputers, about 250 medium-size systems and 100 large computers, in addition to 5000 microcomputers. Abicomp optimism was justified on the grounds that small businesses were now using computers, since new desk-top high performance and cheap microcomputers have made feasible the use of electronic data processing. In addition, the banking sector was increasingly using automation throughout its branches. This involved extensive use of minicomputers and terminals.

In 1980 Cobra became the new market leader with about 40 per cent of business minicomputer placements. Labo was the second largest supplier with a 20 per cent share of the minicomputer market. SID held a 15 per cent share, with two other Brazilian manufacturers together accounting for a 19 per cent share (see Table 6.8).

At the end of 1980 there were 1880 minicomputers and over 3000 microcomputers installed by Brazilian manufacturers. Cobra installed more than 60 per cent of them, due to its early market entry (see Table 6.9).

With the entrance of new competitors such as Scopus, Prologica

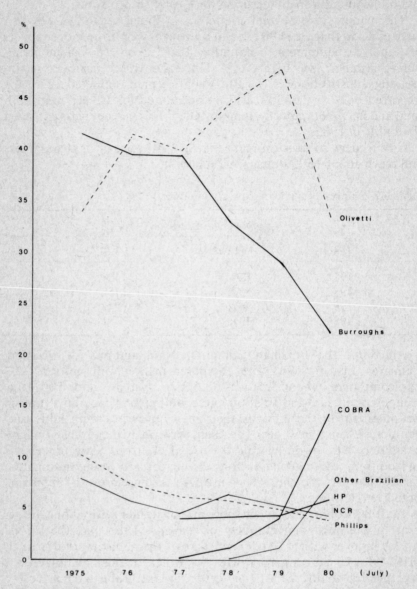

Fig. 6.9 Percentage of minicomputers installed per manufacturer, 1975–80

Table 6.8 Sales of micro and minicomputers per manufacturer 1979–80 (percentage of total sales)

Firm	Minicomputers[a]				Microcomputers[b]			
	Business		Data entry		Business		Data entry	
	1979	1980	1979	1980	1979	1980	1979	1980
Cobra	52.1	38.9	–	–	66.7	63.3	99.5	79.6
Labo	10.9	20.2	13.7	100.0	–	–	–	–
SID	18.0	15.6	86.3	–	–	–	–	–
Edisa	14.6	15.2	–	–	–	–	–	17.6
Sisco	2.2	6.2	–	–	33.3	2.0	–	–
Medidata	2.2	3.9	–	–	–	–	–	–
Polymax	–	–	–	–	–	34.7	–	–
Embracomp	–	–	–	–	–	–	0.5	2.4
BK	–	–	–	–	–	–	–	0.4

Source: Digibras (1981).

[a]Price ranging from US $100 000 to US $200 000. Group 1, Digibras classification.
[b]Price ranging from US $10 000 to US $56 000. Group 2, Digibras classification.

Table 6.9 Micro and minicomputers installed per manufacturer (end of 1980)

Firm	Minicomputers				Microcomputers			
	Business		Data entry		Business		Data entry	
	Q	%	Q	%	Q	%	Q	%
Cobra	1199	66.3	–	–	300	53.8	2399	86.6
Labo	226	12.5	46	64.8	–	–	–	–
SID	153	8.5	25	35.2	–	–	–	–
Edisa	146	8.1	–	–	–	–	307	11.1
Sisco	45	2.5	–	–	15	2.7	–	–
Medidata	40	2.1	–	–	–	–	–	–
Polymax	–	–	–	–	242	43.5	–	–
Embracomp	–	–	–	–	–	–	64	2.3
Total	1809	100.0	71	100.0	557	100.0	2770	100.0

Source: Digibras (1981).

and Dismac, increasing competition can be anticipated in the micro-computer market. Also mini-makers like SID, Labo and Sisco moved down the market in order to include microcomputers in their product range. Tables 6.10 and 6.11 show the range of small business computers and process-control systems manufactured in Brazil respectively.

Table 6.10 Small business computer systems manufactured in Brazil 1981

Manufacturer	Microcomputers up to 64 kb RAM	Minicomputers from 64 to 512 K	Mid-range computers (512 to 2 MB)
Cobra	Cobra 300 (48 K) Cobra 305 (64 K)	Cobra 400 (64 K) Cobra 400 II	Cobra 530 (128–512 K) 1 MB version[a]
Labo	Micro (64 K)[a]	8034 (64–256 K)	8038(512 K)[a] 8043 (1 MB)[a]
Edisa	ED 301 (24–56 K) ED 281 (64–208 K)	ED 311 (32–64 K)	
SID	SID 3000 (64 K)	SID 5000 (64–128)	SID 5800 (up to 1 MB)
Sisco	SCC 5000 (8–32 K)	MB 8000 (65–128 K)	MC 9700 (512 K)[a]
Prologica	Sistema 700 (64 K)		
Scopus	Microscopus (64 K)		
Polymax	Poly 101 (64 K)		
Hewlett-Packard	HP 85 (64 K)		
Novadata	Novadata (96 K)[a]		
Digirrede	UCP (banking)		
Quartzil	QI 800		
Dismac	D 8000 (48 K)		

[a]Under development.

(c) Peripheral equipment

In 1980 the value of sales of peripheral equipment by Brazilian manufacturers, $81.1 million; was a 377 per cent increase over the 1979 sales level of $21.7 million. This was because 1980 was the first year of full manufacturing activities for most firms. Figure 6.10 shows the value of sales in US $ millions for each equipment.

Up to 1977 there were 12 firms marketing 44 models of electronic accounting machines in Brazil. These included NCR, Burroughs (L series), Olivetti (Audit), RUF, Friden, National, Olympia, and Simpro. Simpro was the only Brazilian firm in the market. Since 1978, when the 'market reserve policy' was introduced, the equipment

Table 6.11 Process control systems manufactured in Brazil 1981

Firm	Basic hardware	Application
Cobra	Cobra 700 TD 100, 200, 300	Industrial process control; SSO—building, electricity, CCO—communication
Sisco	IND 5005	Industrial and scientific applications, control and supervision
	5400 Serie	Industrial control
	5500 Serie	Telecontrol
Elebra Electronica	MAP	Telecontrol and supervision Process control Numerical control

has been manufactured and designed locally by Brazilian firms only. Three foreign firms—Olivetti, RUF and Friden—sell equipment manufactured by local firms under their own brand names. Table 6.12 shows electronic accounting machines produced in Brazil per manufacturer.

Tables 6.13, 6.14 and 6.15 shows terminals, printers and magnetic storage devices manufactured in Brazil. They estimate the quantity of equipments produced in 1981.

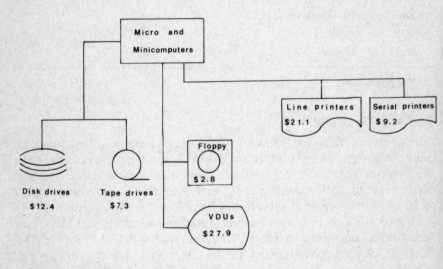

Source: Digibrás

Fig. 6.10 Sales of peripherals by Brazilian manufacturers, 1980 (US $ million)

Table 6.12 Electronic accounting machines manufactured in Brazil, 1981

Firm	Equipment
Dismac	KC 7000 (being phased-out) Alfa 2038/48 Alfa 2064
Exata	EX 4000, EX 4800
Prologica	MCA-12 MCA-100 MCA-24 (commercialized by Olivetti and RUF)
Sharp	800

(d) Software

It is difficult to evaluate the Brazilian market for computer software services, as there has been little data gathered. However, research into the American market shows that software is absorbing an increasing share in the total cost of a computer system. It is foreseen that, in 1985, software will represent more than 80 per cent of the total system cost (see Figure 6.11).

The sharp increase in demand for software services is supporting the development of independent software houses which provide application software products and consultancy services. This tendency has been observed in Brazil since the introduction of minicomputers. A typical minicomputer customer has no previous experience in data processing. They would rather buy complete application packages than invest in specialized personnel to supply their software needs. Minicomputer manufacturers offer a set standard application software. But they lack the financial resources and the expertise to develop a wide range of software products. Most computer manufacturers are already spending more than 50 per cent of their R & D budget on software development. In 1981 they developed in-house more than 80 per cent of the software services they needed against only 40 per cent in 1979 (see Figure 6.12). Minicomputers are also moving towards independent software and system houses to obtain additional help in software development.[2] Officially registered software services imports, however, have decreased steadily since 1979.

With programming becoming increasingly important in system development, independent software suppliers, known as system

[2] See paper presented at SBC conference by Luiz de Castro Martins. In *Datanews*, 15 July 1981, p. 24.

Table 6.13 Terminals manufactured in Brazil, 1981

Firm	VDUs and data entry	Bank terminals	Point-of-sale terminals
CMA	VDO 8500		
Cobra	TR 100, 200 STV 1600 TD 100, 200	TCB	PDV (48 K)
Digilab		Teller system Electronic bank equipment	
Digirrede		Bank terminal[a]	
Dismac	D-8000 (16 K) personal computer	Bank terminal[a]	
Edisa	ED 100 (Data entry) ED 112	ED	
ELO Informatica	Sistema 32 Spooler (Data entry)		
Embracomp	SDE 41 Data entry TB 110, TS[a] BT 52 Data terminal[a]		
IBM do Brasil	3274/76 Control unit 3278 Video 3297 Colour video		
Itautec		Terminals Concentrators	

Labo	Data entry		
NCR do Brasil			NCR 2125[a]
OZ Eletronica		Moddata MT 2000	
Parks	Video terminal		
Polymax	Poly 101[b]		
Racimec		Datatronic	PS terminal[a]
Scopus	TVA 32, 80, 800, 1000 PC 2100 Communicator		
SID	Data entry	Bank terminal	
Sisco	TV 2000, TIC 9000 DE 5000 Data entry		
Tecnodata			TC 21/18 (16 K) TCR 26/40
Zanthus		Z–2000	
Estimated quantity of equipment manufactured in 1981[d]	10 500	10 000	

[a] Under development.
[b] Part of a word processor system.
[c] NCR had a local manufacturing plan approved in May 1981 on condition that they exported two-thirds of total output.
[d] Source: *Datanews*.

Table 6.14 Printers produced in Brazil per manufacturer and estimated 1981 output

	Printers	
Manufacturer	Serial	Matrix
Burroughs	Low-speed printer mechanisms	750 to 1500 1 pm
Digilab	–	300, 600 and 1200[a] 1pm
Elebra Informa.	100 CPS (Emilia), 160 CPS	–
Elgin Maquinas	–	Matrix printer[a]
Globus	100 CPS, 200 CPS	300, 600, 900, 1200 1pm
IBM	Bahia (for export only)	
Polymax	90 CPS[b]	
Embracom	–	50-100 1pm
Estimated 1981 output	4850 units	

[a]Under development.
[b]Uses Burroughs printer mechanism.

Table 6.15 Magnetic storage devices produced in Brazil and estimated 1981 output

	Magnetic storage devices			
Manufacturer	Tape drives	Cassette	Disk drives	Floppy disk
Burroughs	–	–	130 MB removable 200/400 MB fixed	–
Elebra INF	–	–	16-80 MB 12 MB	0.4-1.6 MB
Globus	25/45 ips 1600 bpi	–	–	–
Microlab	1600 bpi	–	10 and 80 MB	5-10 MB[a b]
Multidigit	–	–	10-20 MB	5-10 MB[a b]
Flexidisk	–	–	5.58 MB fixed[b]	5¼"
Racimec	–	Build-in	–	–
Compart	12.5/37.5/45 ips	–	–	–
Estimated 1981 output	2017	–	3311	8700

[a]Under development.
[b]Utilizes Winchester technology.

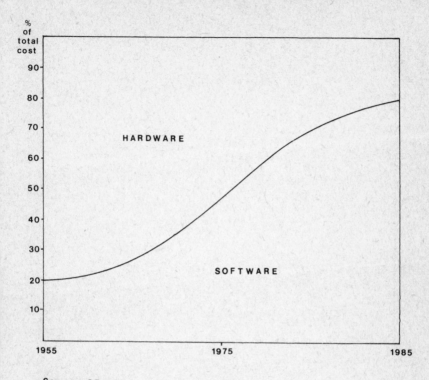

Source: SEI

Fig. 6.11 Relationship between the cost of software and hardware in a computer system

houses, are gaining increasing importance in the computer industry. System houses usually buy or rent hardware from computer manufacturers and supply it to end-users, providing all software services, including tests and compilation.

In 1981 there were 88 software houses in Brazil developing application software for local minicomputer manufacturers. They have already produced 230 packages, most of them oriented towards business applications (accounting, pay roll management, stock control, etc.).

Software houses in Brazil compete directly with foreign software suppliers, as software packages can be imported freely. Software imports are very difficult to control. A complete package can be brought into the country on magnetic tapes, disks or even cassette tapes, and thus be reproduced and sold locally. SEI is now studying measures to protect local software houses. These include the registration of software imports as technology imports, and 'market reserve' for local firms in some areas of software development.

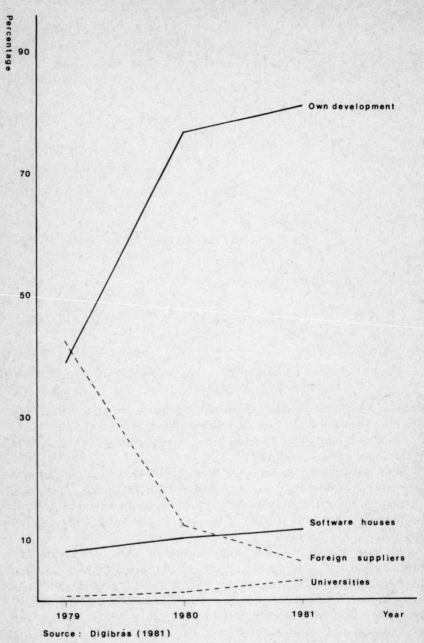

Source: Digibrás (1981)

Fig. 6.12 Source of software services utilized by Brazilian computer manufacturers (percentage of total expenditure on software services)

Some large multinational firms are placing more and more software programs into the hardware itself—chips which come to be called 'firmware'. This can have implications on the future of independent software houses.

4   THE EMERGENCE OF A COMPUTER POLICY IN BRAZIL

The emergence of a national policy in Brazil dates from the early 1970s. The increasing use of computers and the availability of high-level scientists and engineers to design and develop some types of computer products lend support to the possibility that Brazil could develop some technological autonomy in the sector. The first attempt to establish an indigenous computer capability was made in March 1971. A contract was signed between a Navy Special Work Group and BNDE (on behalf of the Ministry of Planning) to set up a project called Funtec 111 with funding of up to US $2 million.[3] Funtec 111 provided financial support for the design of the mini-computer G-10, undertaken by two Brazilian universities.

Capre (Coordenacao das Atividades de Processamento Eletronico) was founded in 1972, and initially concentrated on encouraging the efficient use of computers in public administration. In the same year Eletronica Digital Brasileira (EDB) was formed. This was a holding company through which BNDE and other public organizations could engage in the formation of computer companies. In 1974 EDB changed its name to Digibras and set up Computadores e Sistemas Brasileiros (Cobra). Cobra was concerned with developing and manufacturing minicomputers locally and had its initial capital subscribed in equal parts by three partners; Digibras, Equipamentos Eletronicos—EE (a Brazilian industrial organization) and the British firm Ferranti Limited. Ferranti was selected as the foreign partner and technology supplier after competing with various international firms including DEC, Hewlett-Packard, Varian, CII, and Fujitsu. At that time Ferranti had already supplied computer-based ship and submarine systems for the Brazilian Navy. Ferranti became a minor shareholder (less than 3 per cent) after subsequent subscription bids because policy makers did not want Cobra attached to a single technology supplier and wanted to avoid foreign control of Cobra's technical decisions. EE shareholding was substituted by other public and private companies due to inadequate availability of funds.

The creation of a 'national champion' has been one of the goals of

---

[3] Cr $10 million at mid-1971 exchange rate of US $1 = Cr $5.

many European government policies in the computer industry. ICL in Britain, CII-HB in France, AEG-Telefunken and lately Nixdorf in Germany have largely benefited from government procurement policy and financial support, in order to balance 'le defi Americain' in the sector. In Brazil this policy has never been explicit. But since the beginning of its operation, Cobra performed the role of 'national champion' and model for the Brazilian computer industry.

Local computer manufacturing by foreign multinationals could, in some cases, be defended theoretically on purely economic terms. In reality, however, it would imply surrendering the development of local technological capabilities in a field which represents the cutting edge of modern industry. A wide cross-section of Brazilian industrial sectors, such as aircraft, automobiles, petrochemicals and steel, had reached a stage of development that required computerized manufacturing techniques—for example, numerically controlled machinery in automotive parts or an automated processing plant—if international competitiveness was to be attained. Also, the development of the internal market for business computers and the availability of local skills to develop and manufacture data-processing equipment made feasible the growth of an independent industry.

The subsidiaries of multinationals which had data-processing equipment manufacturing activities in Brazil due to the centralization of research and development (R & D) activities in their home countries were not interested in either developing or absorbing local product development efforts. IBM, for example, carried out R & D activities outside the USA, but the primary purpose of overseas R & D centres was to absorb specific skills from local high-level engineers and scientists who were unwilling to work in the USA. The IBM Technology Unit located in Zurich, Switzerland, for example, was created in order to utilize outstanding European scientists to investigate the possibility of using magnetic film to replace magnetic cores in computer memories (Ronstadt, 1977). Considering the relatively low availability of computer technologists in Brazil, it was quite unlikely that significant R & D activities would be carried out by the corporation in that country.

The development of Brazilian firms concerned with developing manufacturing and marketing data-processing equipment soon faced the situation of having to compete directly with the subsidiaries of large MNCs which supplied the local market. The presence of these subsidiaries as well-established computer suppliers represented a barrier to entry for local firms and inhibited private or public efforts to develop an independent industry.

The experience of other countries, such as Japan and some Western European countries[4] showed that protectionism from both imports and local manufacturing by MNCs' subsidiaries was required in developing an independent computer industry. In Brazil control over computer imports began in 1975. It was introduced by Capre due to the need to reduce imports and to create policy instruments for the development of a local computer industry. In the following year Capre became responsible for formulating policies for fostering national computer industries.

In July 1976 Capre announced an industrial policy for mini-computers and auxiliary equipment. This included the search for increasing applications for local technology and the involvement of local firms in manufacturing. Because of the high cost and technological requirements involved in the development and manu-facture of large computers the policy was basically concerned with the use of imported products.

In 1977 Capre invited firms wishing to manufacture minicomputers in Brazil to submit their plans. Capre's approval was a precondition for obtaining an import licence for component parts. There were five criteria for assessing firms' manufacturing plans:

1 Priority would be given to firms which intended to utilize local technological resources to design and develop computer products. Technology transfer agreements with foreign firms would be allowed. But recipient firms should display a capacity to learn foreign know-how and not become dependent on foreign partners in the long term for technology, management and other skills.
2 Degree of incorporation of locally manufactured components. This was justified not only on economic terms (foreign currency savings), but also by the fact that intensive utilization of local components represented a technical capacity to adapt designs to local conditions.
3 Firms' market shares. Capre wanted to avoid excessive market concentration such as that prevailing in the large and very large computer market where a single firm held about 70 per cent of the total installed base.
4 Local partnership—firms incorporating a majority of local capital would be given priority.
5 Foreign trade balance. Subsidiaries of MNCs usually showed better export performance than locally owned firms. But MNCs tended to import most components needed in a computer system and

[4] See Jequier, Nicholas, 'Computers' in Vernon, R. (1974) and Canada, Science Council, *Strategies of Development for the Canadian Computer Industry*.

to incur higher deficits on service bills (royalties and technical assistance), and capital remittance (profits, interest rates).

Four locally owned firms were thus selected to manufacture mini-computers in Brazil. They were chosen out of 16 firms, of which seven were subsidiaries of MNCs, two were joint-ventures and seven were locally owned. The same criteria were applied in following years to select manufacturers for other data-processing equipment such as printers, disk and tape drives, microcomputers, electronic accounting machines, modems and terminals. The policy of selecting a number of firms to manufacture specific computer products became known as the 'market reserve policy'. The main advantages of this policy were to overcome the barriers to entry established by computer multinationals in Brazil and to enable the application of local technical inputs.

By the end of 1979 some reorganization of government bodies responsible for the computer sector took place. A new agency called Secretaria Especial de Informatica (SEI) took over Capre's activities. It was responsible to the National Security Council while Capre was under the Ministry of Planning. Despite the widespread substitution of top and middle rank officials, SEI has kept the same basic policy with respect to manufacture of computers. SEI increased its range of activities to include other industrial sectors such as microelectronics, communications equipment and instruments.

Government policies for computers in Brazil had an important impact on both local and foreign corporate strategies. In product policy where technology transfer agreements were not encouraged, local firms were influenced to undertake their own product development. Foreign shareholdings in local firms were kept to a minimum and manufacturers were pushed to increase rapidly the content of locally manufactured components.

MNCs also had to modify their corporate policies in Brazil. Firms which already had an established industrial base in Brazil —such as IBM and Burroughs—had to embark on a large export drive in order to be allowed to launch new products in the internal market. The opportunities for new entrants, however, were limited primarily to technology transfers because of the protection enjoyed by the local small computer and peripheral equipment suppliers.

5 THE DEVELOPMENT OF DESIGN CAPABILITIES IN
   BRAZILIAN FIRMS

Spin-off companies

The pioneer work on computer research in Brazil was done by government institutions. The main goal of the research activities was to train indigenous manpower to make better use of the imported equipment rather than to design and develop data-processing equipment locally. Nevertheless, some products were successfully developed in the early 1970s. These included the G-10 minicomputer developed jointly by the University of São Paulo (USP) and Rio de Janeiro Catholic University (PUC); the keyboard concentrator developed by Serpro; and the intelligent terminal developed by Rio de Janeiro Federal University (UFRJ). At least four spin-off computer manufacturers originated from the capabilities acquired in these design projects (see Figure 6.13).

Serpro is a state enterprise responsible for services using data processing such as tax receipts and payment of civil servants. It is the largest computer user in Latin America. Serpro's involvement with the development and manufacturing of data-processing equipment was a result of its own demand for some particular equipment which was not available on the international market. The income tax processing service, for example, required the intensive use of data-entry equipment. The most suitable system for this service, according to Serpro technicians, was a set of keyboards linked to a main storage system (tape or disk drive). Since data-entry operations involve many errors, data-entry equipment requires error-detection devices. The input capacity of each keyboard is determined by the typing speed of each individual keyboard operator. This is much lower than the data-acquisition capacity of the storage system. Consequently, an efficient data-entry system should include a concentration device to link the input data from many keyboards and thus balance the dataflow towards the storage system.

In 1970 Serpro sought such a system but could not find a suitable one in the international market. At the time there was no local firm with the necessary skills to undertake the system development. Therefore, Serpro decided to set up its own facilities to design, develop and manufacture a keyboard concentrator and other equipment. In the same year Serpro started to develop a system involving a 48K on-line microcomputer linked with up to 32 keyboard terminals. More than 50 systems involving 1200 terminals had been

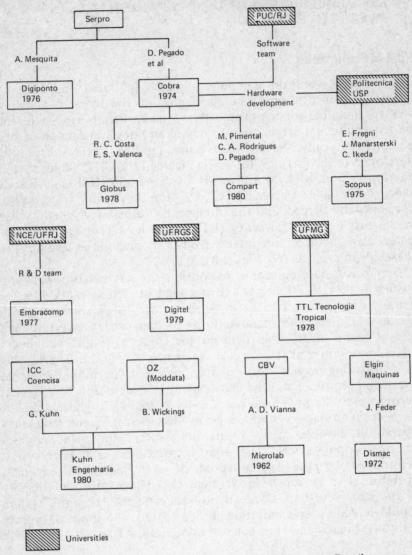

Fig. 6.13 Spin-off DP equipment manufacturers in Brazil

built up to 1975. In addition, other data-entry models were developed by Serpro's Manufacturing Division.

With the establishment of Cobra in the mid-1970s, Serpro transferred to it its data-entry manufacturing operations and the bulk of its research and development technicians, including the Manufacturing Division manager who became the technical director of Cobra.

Serpro's technology formed the base for a number of Cobra's product lines. These included remote terminals, data terminals (TD 100, 200) and data-entry systems.

An electronic keyboard unit was another important product development undertaken by Serpro. This product had been manufactured in-house up to 1975 after which it was no longer required internally due to the transfer to Cobra of Serpro's manufacturing operations. Cobra did not want to expand vertically into components. This gave the opportunity for three engineers involved in the keyboard project to establish a private firm called Digiponto to take over the manufacturing of electronic keyboards. Serpro transferred to the new firm all designs, technical data, tools and key-top moulds and Digiponto became the first Brazilian electronic keyboard manufacturer.

The development of the G-10 minicomputer, jointly undertaken by USP (hardware) and PUC (software), also gave rise to a spin-off company. In 1975 a group of engineers involved in the G-10's hardware development left USP to found the private firm Scopus. Based on its relatively high hardware development capabilities, Scopus became Brazil's leading manufacturer of CRT terminals and related equipment.

The G-10 development reinforced Cobra's capabilities. In 1977 the company took over the responsibility for further development of the minicomputer. At that time PUC closed down its Computer Design Laboratory and most of the technical personnel involved in software development continued to work on this project at Cobra. Cobra also took on two engineers from USP who had worked on G-10's hardware design.

Cobra gave rise to spin-off companies downstream. In 1978 peripheral equipment manufacturer Globus was founded by two ex-directors of Cobra in association with an entrepreneurial group. About 80 per cent of Globus' managerial staff came from Cobra. In 1980 a change in Cobra's board of directors produced another spin-off firm, manufacturing magnetic tape drives, called Compart. The firm was founded by the ex-president and two ex-directors of Cobra, including the technical director.

The activities of the computer centre of Rio de Janeiro Federal University (NCE/UFRJ) also resulted in the spin-off of a manufacturing firm. In 1977, after successfully completing the development of CRT and intelligent terminals, NCE's engineers and technicians were frustrated by the lack of industry interest in undertaking further development and manufacture of these products. At this time there was no protection for the Brazilian computer industry and the market was supplied by MNCs. NCE personnel themselves decided to set up a manufacturing firm. Embracomp, was founded with initial capital subscribed by 69 NCE employees, including engineers, technicians and administrative staff.

Two modem manufacturers—TTL (Tecnologia Tropical) and Digitel—were established by technologists from the electronic departments of Minas Gerais and Rio Grande do Sul Federal Universities respectively.

There are three main examples of spin-offs from manufacturing firms. In 1962 Microlab was founded based on the Nuclear and Electronics divisions of CBV. The firm originally began as a telecommunications laboratory, but in 1973 it began manufacturing activities. Dismac was founded in 1972 following a spin-off from Elgin Maquinas. The firm began producing mini-calculators but in 1978 it began manufacturing electronic accounting machines. A third spin-off company was the result of the association of engineers from two modems manufacturing firms. Called Kuhn Engenharia, it was set up in 1980 and produces modem equipment. Spin-off companies had a positive influence on the technological development of the Brazilian computer industry. They contributed to the spread of the limited technical capability developed in local data-processing research centres. In general, they pursued autonomous product and process design.

'New business projects'

'New business projects' are defined as those ventures established by entrepreneurs with no previous experience in electronics. Involvement in data-processing equipment manufacturing was the result of a policy of diversification. These entrepreneurs were able to obtain the necessary skills to develop and manufacture computer products.

The main example of a 'new business project' is the system manufacturer Polymax. It was set up by a food-processing industry entrepreneur with technical support from Procergs, the data-processing service company of the State of Rio Grande do Sul. Polymax undertook product development in-house.

Other firms stemming from non-related industrial sectors are Digilab (Abramo Eberle Steel and Bradesco), Multidigit (Cataguases Light and Power) and Flexidisk (IBCT). 'New business projects' had the advantage of bringing managerial expertise to the computer manufacturing sector. This may have contributed to increasing the level of competition within the industry.

Technical entrepreneurs

Many firms were established by electronic engineers who took the decision to develop and manufacture data-processing equipment. In general, they were small firms oriented towards microcomputer development. Some examples are Exata, Digirede, Medidata, Prologica, Gepeto and Novadata. In general, such firms are 'innovators' and rely on their own product development to secure a market entry.

Firms with previous experience in electronics

Some firms had previous experience in electronics but in fields other than data-processing equipment. From 1977, when government policy explicitly favoured local firms, they began to manufacture computer products as well. Examples of these firms are Elebra Electronica, Racimec, Labo Electronica, Micolab, J. C. Melo and Sharp Group. Firms with previous manufacturing facilities in electronics may have contributed to the vertical integration of the computer industry. The also brought manufacturing expertise to the sector.

7 COMPETITIVE BEHAVIOUR IN THE BRAZILIAN COMPUTER INDUSTRY

1 INTRODUCTION

This chapter will analyse the competitive behaviour of Brazilian computer firms. This includes evaluating the main competitive elements in that industry, the role of direct and indirect competition with multinationals, advantages and disadvantages of joint ventures with foreign firms, and the export potential of indigenous data-processing (DP) equipment manufacturers. It will be testing some of the hypotheses set up in Part One.[1]

2 COMPETITIVE ADVANTAGES AND DISADVANTAGES

Firms' competitive behaviour is usually related to market conditions and perceptions of their competitive advantages and disadvantages. This study found four major competitive elements in the Brazilian computer market: product design, marketing strength, financial resources, and technical capabilities. It was found that manufacturing technology has not yet become a major competitive element, since the sector is still in a stage of batch production. Manufacturing technology may have a very important role in competition in the near future as the scale of production increases and with the development of automated process technology including automatic insertion, automatic testing and robotics.

Product design concerns the quality and performance of the equipment. Marketing strength refers to the effectiveness of the distribution system and services provided for customers. Financial resources involve firms' capacity to invest in R & D, manufacturing and marketing. Finally, technical capabilities concern firms' capacity

[1] The analysis is based on information collected directly from 23 locally owned data-processing equipment manufacturers which accounted for about 90 per cent of total sales of DP equipment manufactured by indigenous firms in 1980. It included statistical methods (Yules' Q and chi-square test) in order to evaluate the correlations between the variables related to competition (see section on Research Methods).

to develop new products and to adapt existing products to the particular needs for the local market.

In general, firms' choice of goals and strategies are based on their perception of their relative strength in each one of these competitive elements. Thus, firms' competitive strategies can be understood by the analysis of their perceived competitive advantages and disadvantages. Table 7.1 summarizes the attitudes of firms about their competitive strengths and weaknesses in the Brazilian computer industry.

Table 7.1 Competitive advantages and disadvantages of Brazilian computer firms

Competitive element	Advantage	Neutral	Disadvantage	Total
Product design	16	6	1	23
Marketing	6	13	4	23
Technical capabilities	6	10	7	23
Financial resources	6	9	8	23

Perception of competitive advantages and disadvantages were statistically analysed in relation to other variables. These included firm size, source of technology, export potential, degree of competition with multinationals, production sector and firm's location. Table 7.2 gives bivariate correlations (Yules' Q) between variables collapsed into dichotomous categories.

Statistical association between dichotomized variables such as A and B exists if, when A occurs it is accompanied relatively more frequently by B than by *not B*. Yules' Q measures statistical association on a scale from $Q = +1$ (perfect association between A and B), through $Q = 0$ (perfect independence of A and B), to $Q = -1$ (perfect dissociation between A and B and by inference, association between A and not B). The correlations were subjected to the chi-square test which evaluates whether or not coefficients obtained empirically by Yules' Q differ significantly from those which would be expected casually.

A basic subdivision into small and medium or large firms has been made, based upon the employment criteria most frequently used in Brazil: 10–99 (small) 100 and over (medium and large). As the weighting coefficients contained in the discriminant function can be interpreted as in multiple regression techniques, they were used to identify those variables which contributed most in differentiating size from other characteristics of firms.

A second distinction was made between firms which license their

Table 7.2 Competitive behaviour correlation matrix

	1 Size	2 Source of tech.	3 Marketing	4 Financial resources	5 Design	6 Tech.	7 Export potential	8 Competition MNCs	9 Production sector	10 Company's location
			Competitive advantage							
1 Size	1	0.412	0.698[a]	0.280	-0.428	-0.176	-0.379	0.538[a]	0.273	0.680[a]
2 Source of technology	0.412	1	0.385	0.385	0.263	-0.058	-0.859[a]	-0.636[a]	-0.555[a]	-0.420
3 Competitive advantage —Marketing	0.698[a]	0.385	1	0.647[a]	-0.091	-0.351	0.529[a]	-0.412	0.803[a]	0.754[a]
4 Competitive advantage —Financial resources	0.280	0.385	0.647[a]	1	-0.529[a]	-1[a]	0.091	0.043	0.059	0.754[a]
5 Competitive advantage —Product design	-0.428	0.263	-0.091	-0.529[a]	1	-0.529[a]	0.064	-0.200	0.525[a]	-0.143
6 Competitive advantage —Technical capabilities	-0.176	-0.058	-0.351	-1[a]	-0.529[a]	1	0.091	0.555	-0.754[a]	-0.803[a]
7 Export potential	-0.379	-0.859[a]	0.529[a]	0.091	0.064	0.091	1	0.643[a]	0.091	-0.263
8 Competition with MNCs	0.538[a]	-0.636[a]	-0.412	0.043	-0.200	0.555	0.643[a]	1	0.311	0.066
9 Production sector	0.273	-0.555[a]	0.803[a]	0.059	0.525[a]	-0.754[a]	0.525	0.311	1	0.420
10 Company's location	0.680[a]	-0.420	0.754[a]	0.754[a]	-0.143	-0.803[a]	-0.263	0.066	0.420	1

[a]Significant correlation.

OBS: Size: Small/medium and large; source of technology: licensing/own development; competitive advantages: marketing (yes/no), financial resources (yes/no), product design (yes/no), technical capabilities (yes/no); export potential: good/bad; competition with multinationals: yes/no; product sectors: system/peripheral; company location: São Paulo/other states.

technology (12 firms) and those which obtain it through other means (11 firms). For product sectors, firms were dichotomized into system (11 firms) and peripheral manufacturers (12 firms). Competitive elements were separated into two groups. The first refers to 'advantages' and the second includes both 'neutral' and 'disadvantages'. Export potential and competition with multinationals will be studied later in this chapter. Location was subdivided into São Paulo based (12 firms) and other states (11 firms). Figure 7.1 further clarifies the way variables were dichotomized.

Product design

Product design, as Table 7.1 shows, is the most commonly perceived competitive advantage among Brazilian computer firms. The computer market is highly imperfect and the pattern of competition is firmly based on product differentiation rather than price. Firms associate their products with real or imagined quality attributes such as superior product designs.

Product competition generally favours foreign subsidiaries supported by their parents' technical assistance and flow of innovation. But locally owned firms which acquired foreign designs through licensing agreements may have important competitive advantages, especially in market segments essentially closed to foreign firms.

Of the 23 firms interviewed, 16 perceived product design as one of their major competitive advantages. Product design was the single advantage for seven of them. Part of the explanation for the importance of product competition lies in the fact that most firms were recently established. Their initial efforts were concentrated on product development or adaptation of licensed products. Since these activities demand high investment, most firms might not have sufficient resources to also become involved in the development of other competitive strategies, such as servicing and marketing networks.

The analysis of correlation coefficients further clarify the relationship between product and other competitive advantages. Negative correlation between strength in product design and financial resources was $Q = -0.529$. This means that firms which had product as a major competitive advantage were seldom strong in financial resources. A second significant negative correlation ($Q = -0.529$) was found between technical capabilities and product design. Firms which had a good product design did not necessarily have outstanding technical capabilities. This can be explained by the relatively large number of firms which acquired a good product design through licensing

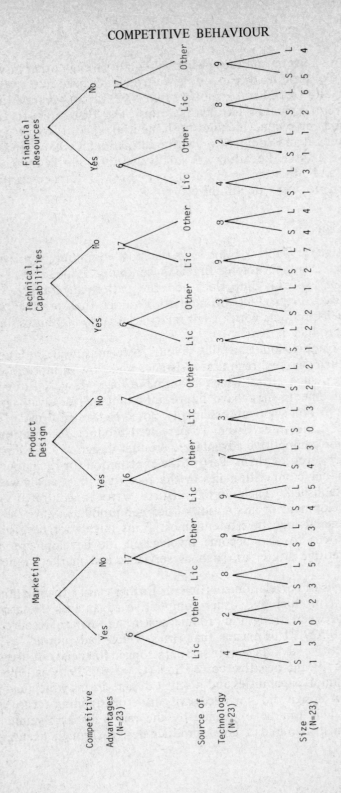

Fig. 7.1

agreements without having developed their own technical capabilities. Finally, competitive product correlated highly with product sector (Q = 0.525). This indicates that system manufacturers enjoyed more advantages in product design than peripheral manufacturers.

Marketing

Firms reported having a competitive advantage in marketing when they had a well-established sales network and were relatively strong with back-up such as software, service and maintenance, as well as pricing and customer financing. Marketing strength is an essential competitive element for manufacturers of products oriented towards the end-user market such as point-of-sales terminals, micro and mini-computers. Peripheral equipment manufacturers, however, do not in general depend so much on marketing capabilities since they usually supply a relatively small number of OEM customers who closely specify their own needs and cost constraints. This can be illustrated by the fairly high correlation between the system product sector and marketing strength (Q = 0.803).

Brazilian system and electronic accounting machine manufacturers employ between 20 and 30 per cent of their total workforce in marketing activities such as sales, maintenance services and support software, while peripheral manufacturers employ only 10 per cent of their workforce in these activities. Table 7.3 shows the distribution of sales between the OEM and user market in Brazil.

Table 7.3 Distribution of sales of Brazilian DP equipment manufacturers according to the type of customer

	Percentage of total turnover	
Type of customer	1978	1979[a]
OEM	27	36
End-user	73	64
Total	100	100

Source: Digibras, *Relatorio Semestral de Marketing*, 1979.

[a] First half.

There is a high correlation between size and marketing strength (Q = 0.698). Large firms have the advantage of gaining access to regional markets by extending their distribution and servicing system. Small firms concentrated their sales efforts in the Rio–São Paulo region where nearly 70 per cent of Brazilian computer customers are located. Only two firms had a nationwide distribution system— Cobra and SID. In 1981 Cobra had 37 servicing and maintenance offices in Brazil. SID had sales and maintenance facilities in all Brazilian state capitals.

The method by which products are marketed plays an important role in firms' marketing strategies. In 1980 three-quarters of data-processing equipment was either leased or rented to customers, while only one-quarter was actually sold. Leasing operations are usually financed by an independent financial institution, while renting is directly sponsored by the computer manufacturer for a period ranging from 35 to 40 months. Renting operations have increased steadily since 1978 (see Table 7.4).

Table 7.4 Forms of commercialization of DP equipment in Brazil

| Year | Percentage of total sales | | | |
	Direct sales	Leasing	Rental	Total
1978	30.6	68.8	0.6	100.0
1979	21.1	73.1	5.8	100.0
1980	23.7	64.6	11.7	100.0
1981[a]	22.5	65.2	12.3	100.0

Source: Digibras.

[a]Forecast

Firms linked to financial institutions which provided leasing services perceived themselves to be particularly strong in marketing. This may be verified by the high correlation found between marketing and financial strength ($Q = 0.647$). Large multinationals were also favoured by this pattern of commercialization, since they had their own often large resources to invest in renting operations.

Most Brazilian computer product manufacturers did not have clear marketing strategies. Many firms chose to operate in the commercial market segment, for example, business microcomputers, without having a clear appreciation of the marketing skills and resources required by this segment of business. Consequently, they were facing increasing difficulties in competition.

Few firms were oriented to the state and special systems market such as process control, scientific equipment and the military market. Although competition in these market segments is determined by product quality rather than marketing strength, the size of the

Brazilian market for special systems might not be large enough to encourage firms to concentrate on it.

Some firms found a way round their lack of marketing resources by entering into sales agreements with local subsidiaries of multi-national firms. These agreements provided an offset for some local firms but they were only a temporary rather than a final solution for their marketing weakness. These agreements were facing opposition from SEI and Abicomp since they represented a loophole in the 'market reserve policy'.

São Paulo-based firms were particularly strong in marketing, since the correlation between a company's location and marketing strength was fairly high (Q = 0.754). This may be explained by the existence of financially strong firms in São Paulo and by the fact that some firms located in this area had previous experience in selling office equipment.

The need to develop marketing capabilities represents a major challenge to the Brazilian computer industry. Local firms not only have to face competition from multinationals in some segments of the market which were not totally protected by the 'market reserve policy', but also have to find new marketing strategies in order to develop the local market. The reduction in prices of mini-computers, for example, may make the use of visiting salesmen uneconomic, since the costs of this method of selling absorb an increasing share of the minicomputer total price. Thus, new forms of commercialization such as 'computer shops' have to be developed in order to minimize sales costs.

Technical capabilities

Six firms perceived that they enjoyed particular strength in technical capabilities which they used to competitive advantage. These firms may be divided into two groups: the first are firms which entered into licensing agreements. They utilized their technical capabilities to absorb foreign technology and acquire the necessary skills to develop their subsequent generation of computer products in-house. The second group involves firms which developed their own product lines. These firms were able to take advantage of their technical capabilities by designing equipment adequate for the needs of local customers. This includes terminals compatible with imported main-frame computers and commercial microcomputers specially designed to match local business practices.

Typically, firms which had technical capabilities as a competitive advantage were peripheral products manufacturers rather than system makers. A negative correlation between product sector and this competitive advantage was found to be significant ($Q = -0.754$). They were usually located out of the São Paulo area. Negative correlation between company location and technical capabilities was $Q = -0.803$. A possible explanation for this is that the establishment of computer firms in São Paulo was encouraged by the business opportunities offered by the local market, the existing industrial and managerial infra-structure and availability of financial resources. Firms located in other regions lacked most of these incentives and location was attributable to the technical capabilities of their entrepreneurs.

Lack of technical capability was perceived as a competitive disadvantage for seven firms. They lacked the skilled personnel to improve the performance of their equipment or to absorb design and development capacity from their licensers. Lack of technical ability imposes a serious challenge to computer firms. On the one hand firms without licensing agreements can be driven out of the market for not keeping up with the increasing quality and performance standards required by the market. On the other hand, licensees without the necessary technical capabilities are likely to remain dependent on licensers for product change and technical decisions.

Financial resources

Access to adequate financial resources is one of the most critical elements in competition. The market for data-processing equipment in Brazil was growing very fast. Consequently, manufacturers demanded an increasing flow of fresh investment in order to expand operations and protect their market shares. The volume of investment required by firms was usually larger than they could finance through revenue generated by the sale of products. Thus they needed additional external financial support.

There are four activities within a DP manufacturing firm which demand an increasing flow of investment. First, the firm must invest heavily in R & D activities, since competitiveness is dependent upon innovation and product differentiation. This includes the development of new applied software. Second, it must expand manufacturing facilities in order to keep its share in a fast-growing market. Third, the firm needs to invest in the expansion and improvement of marketing services such as customer financing, sales support and maintenance services. Fourth, the computer business in Brazil depends upon ever-expanding working capital requirements because it relies on expensive imported components which are taxed in advance.

In the Brazilian computer industry the major source of financial resources is direct investment by shareholders including undistributed profit. Fourteen firms, accounting for two-thirds of the sample, cited this as their major source of finance. The second source of investment was customer financing. Four firms said they relied on advance payments from customers for developing special products. Credit was the least-cited source of investment (only 14 per cent of the sample; see Table 7.5).

Table 7.5 Major source of financial resources in the Brazilian computer industry

Major source of financial resources	Firms	% of total
Shareholders	14	66.7
Customers	4	19.0
Credit	3	14.3
Total	21	100.0

Adequate financial resources were perceived as a competitive advantage for six firms. They were linked to large industrial or financial groups, including commercial banks. These groups provided steady infusions of new capital, which were essential for preserving and expanding market shares. The growth of these firms would have been limited if they had to rely only on internal funds.

Financially strong firms were usually strong in marketing as well ($Q = 0.647$). They did not rely so much on product design as a competitive advantage. There was significant negative correlation between this and financial strength ($Q = -0.529$).

For eight firms the financial situation was perceived as a competitive disadvantage. Financial difficulties affected two important competitive factors: marketing and time of delivery. Marketing operations were affected because firms did not have sufficient resources to invest in advertising, servicing and customer financing. Time of delivery was generally too long because of the lack of working capital to build up an adequate stock of components. Also, the output was usually small, since the firms lacked capital to invest in more capital goods and fixed assets. Financial weakness can be a serious challenge to computer firms, even for those with good products and technical abilities. In time of recession, credit becomes difficult and expensive. The servicing of the firms' debt can thus absorb a high proportion of their income and consequently obstruct firms' growth. Financial difficulties affects long-term planning. Firms running out of cash usually adopt short-term survival strategies neglecting product development and planning.

3 COMPETITION WITH MULTINATIONALS

In theory, Brazilian data-processing equipment manufacturers are protected from foreign competition—both from imports and from the establishment of local subsidiaries by MNCs—by the 'market reserve policy'. In practice, however, almost two-thirds of local firms have faced competition with large MNCs in the Brazilian market. This includes direct local manufacturing by foreign firms, imports, and sales agreements between MNCs' subsidiaries and local manufacturers (see Table 7.6).

Table 7.6 Locally owned firms facing competition with foreign computer and peripheral companies

Type of foreign competition	Locally owned firms facing competition	% of total
Direct manufacturing	8	36.4
Imports	2	9.1
Sales agreements	4	18.1
None	8	36.4
Total	22	100.0

There were four main computer products manufactured locally by subsidiaries of MNCs in competition with products manufactured by locally owned firms. They were video display units (VDUs), microcomputers, printers and mid-range computers.

VDUs were already manufactured in Brazil by IBM when the 'market reserve policy' came into effect. Three Brazilian firms—Embracomp, Scopus and Cobra—produce IBM-compatible VDUs. The Brazilian market for this equipment is estimated at 10 500 units per year. Out of this, more than 70 per cent is a captive market within IBM itself, because of the SNA—Systems Network Architecture—which requires the use of tools only available to IBM. Brazilian terminals are linked to IBM computers via modem by the Binary Synchronous Code (BSC) protocol. But IBM have introduced a new control unit (370 X) which requires a protocol (SDLC) only available in IBM terminals.

IBM imposes barriers to entry into a large proportion of the terminals market through product differentiation. It utilizes its control over the existing computer market to keep control over the peripheral market. Also, it utilizes secret know-how as a barrier to entry. IBM's business practices world-wide have been investigated by American and EEC anti-trust authorities. In December 1980, after more than six years of investigations, the EEC filed a 'statement of objections' against IBM in which, among other demands, the EEC wanted IBM to stop including a minimum amount of main memory in processor prices, to make more systems software freely available to plug-compatible manufacturers, and to provide interface information earlier than at present (*Computer Weekly*, 25 December 1980, p. 24).

Another important barrier to entry for local firms results from the well-established position of IBM in the Brazilian market. Customers' preferences are established due to goodwill, the effect of IBM brand name, loyalty or simply inertia. A computer centre manager reported that there were three different brands of VDU installed in the centre: IBM, Cobra and Scopus. He said that there were no differences in quality or performance between brands. But operators' preference was strongly oriented towards IBM equipment. The operators would only use the Brazilian terminals when all IBM equipment was already being taken up.

The dominant position enjoyed by IBM in the Brazilian VDU market strongly supports the hypothesis (Hyp. 1.2) that *Direct investment by multinational firms in developing countries restrains competition and imposes oligopolistic barriers to entry for indigenous firms.*

Microcomputers are manufactured locally by Hewlett-Packard. HP competes only indirectly with local firms, since its microcomputer (HP-85) was oriented towards scientific and technical applications. Printers are manufactured by IBM and Burroughs. Both are in competition with local products. Mid-range and large computers are produced locally by IBM, Burroughs and Honeywell-Bull (in joint venture with a local group). These indirectly compete with Brazilian computers.

Two Brazilian data-processing equipment manufacturers were competing against imported products. Import duties for electronic keyboards in Brazil were only 15 per cent and the imported product could compete in price with local manufacturers. Another firm which produces minicomputers for industrial process found that whole systems were imported in 'package deals' for the petrochemical steel and electricity industries. Those packages included financial arrangements and a wide range of technical inputs. Although the local industry was able to supply many of the process-control systems required in new plants, the systems were imported because of the 'packaged' form in which the agreements were arranged.

Another form of competition between local and foreign firms in the microcomputer market is through sales agreements. Some multinationals which had their plans for local manufacturing turned down by the government, asked local firms to manufacture products on an exclusive basis, and began to sell them under their own brand name.

It is difficult for a buyer to evaluate accurately computer performance because of the complexity of the machine. Consequently, customers tend to give preference to international companies which enjoy goodwill. As Brock (1975) said:

Computer performance is a composite of many different operations: arithmetic functions, compares and program transfers, input-output operations, operating system functions, etc. Different computers are likely to work in a different order on the various functions making up computer performance. For example, one computer is likely to have the best processing speed, one the best input-output capacity, and another the best operating system. Any measure of computer performance must be a weighted average of the different characteristics.

4 ADVANTAGES AND DISADVANTAGES OF JOINT VENTURES

In general, firms were established under a government policy which did not encourage joint ventures. Consequently, they developed their own operational and administrative structure and often in-house capabilities to design and develop computer products. Brazilian computer firms did not have a single clear perspective towards joint ventures with foreign firms.

Most local firms believed that joint ventures would result in technological dependence. They felt that foreign partners usually had greater access to the technical inputs required to manufacture computer products and thus they were likely to play a dominant role. Joint ventures were seen as an association between local managerial and foreign technical resources. Most local entrepreneurs considered that this kind of association might be advantageous when the local partner had not yet committed itself to technology. Under these circumstances local firms could become dependent on large foreign firms and obtain profits by manufacturing established product lines. However, when local firms had already committed themselves to the development of their own design, development and manufacturing capacity, joint ventures were not seen as advantageous.

This can be illustrated by the example of a local peripheral equipment manufacturer. They would not accept a foreign partner in the
peripheral business, since they had already acquired the technical
and managerial resources to run the manufacturing operations.
However, the holding company which owned the firm acquired a
majority share in a local subsidiary of a large Japanese communication-
equipment manufacturer. The Brazilian group had little previous
experience in the technology utilized by the Japanese and was likely
only to play a passive role in product policy and technical decisions.

This suggests that even majority local partnership in overseas subsidiaries of MNCs does not necessarily enable local control over
policies and operations or technology transfer (Hyp. 2.2).

Table 7.7 summarizes the perception of the managers of Brazilian
data-processing equipment manufacturers about the advantages of
entering into joint ventures with foreign firms. Of 14 firms in the
sample, half considered that there were no major advantages in joint
ventures with multinationals once technological developments were
undertaken.

Table 7.7 Advantages of joint ventures with foreign firms

Type of advantage	Firms	% of total
None	7	50.0
Access to an export market	3	21.4
Access to technology	1	7.1
Access to capital	1	7.1
Access to component supply source	1	7.1
Business opportunity	1	7.1
Total	14	100.0

(a) Access to an export market

Three firms argued that the main advantage of entering into joint
ventures with large foreign firms was gaining access to an export
market. They believed that for the foreign partners benefit could
accrue from the cost advantages of undertaking some of the labour-
intensive phases of production in Brazil. So, local joint plants would
be allocated sub-contracting orders.

One entrepreneur believed that if his firm entered into a joint
venture with its American technology supplier, it could take over
the manufacturing of mature products which were being phased
out in US plants. He argued that his partner needed to introduce new
products in the USA in order to keep up with competition. Since

their manufacturing facilities were not large enough to produce both new and traditional product lines, the American firm would have to either expand its own plants or transfer the production of mature products to another firm. If the second option was more attractive, the Brazilian joint venture might gain access to product lines with declining but still large export markets.[2]

(b) Access to technology

One firm expected extra help for improving process technology if it entered into a joint venture with its licenser. Most firms, however, considered that there were no technological advantages in doing so. Existing technology transfer agreements provided all the information required to manufacture computer products.

When the technology supplier was also a large shareholder, the licensed firm was denied the right to enter into licensing agreements with other firms. The licensed firm was tied to its foreign partner with respect to technology sources. Difficulties arising from having a fixed technology supplier can be illustrated by the experience of two Brazilian peripheral equipment manufacturers. The first was a wholly locally owned firm which had a licensing agreement with a European MNC involving the manufacture of computer printers. By the end of 1979 the product under the agreement was no longer competitive, since international competitors launched similar products at significantly lower prices. The Brazilian firm decided to shift to another supplier for kits and components, but finally decided to keep the existing agreement after obtaining significant price reductions on the current printer model. The manager interviewed argued that he would not obtain the same price reduction if his firm were a joint venture.

The second firm was a modem manufacturer partly owned by a multinational firm. The firm found that the foreign partner played a negative role with respect to the development of technical skills within the joint company. The foreign partner was only interested in selling kits and components and did not want to duplicate efforts in design and development. Despite the foreign partner having developed more advanced products, it imposed products which were no longer competitive. The local firm found that it could obtain better deals with alternative international firms if it were independent. The local partner was struggling to keep the firm's R & D activities and diversification policy. The foreign partner, however, wanted the

---

[2] This falls in the theoretical framework of Vernon's product cycle.

firm to give up the development of new products and only manufacture products developed by them in the USA.

No evidence was found in this study to support the hypothesis (Hyp. 2.1) that majority local ownership in overseas subsidiaries facilitates technology transfer through access to technical knowledge generated abroad. On the contrary, the pattern of technical cooperation between local and foreign partners lends support to the alternative hypothesis (Hyp. 2.2) that even majority local partnership in overseas subsidiaries of MNCs does not favour technology transfer.

(c) Access to capital

One firm found that access to capital was the main advantage of joint ventures with multinationals. Other firms, however, perceived the better financial position of foreign partners as a threat, possibly a risk of complete take over. Typically, local partners cannot afford to keep up with the investment volume of their foreign partners. Consequently, they may lose control of the joint venture company in following subscription bids.

(d) Access to components supply

One local manufacturer found that joint-venture firms had better access to components supply than independent firms. This experience, however, was not shared by many other firms interviewed. One firm found that its foreign partner had a tendency to overcharge for the supply of components. The firm could obtain better prices by adopting an independent procurement policy. It gave up buying some components from its overseas partner and was obtaining them from local importers under far better conditions.

Another firm found that dependence on licensers in procurement operations was not a sound policy. Therefore, it planned to either establish its own buying office in the USA or contract an independent procurement firm in that country.

5   EXPORT POTENTIAL

Ability to export is an important factor in the long-term survival of computer firms. Exports enable larger economies of scale in manufacturing and R & D and may enable the growth of firms beyond the limits of the local market.

In Brazil, at the time of this study, only 30 per cent of the 23 locally owned firms interviewed had potential to export more than 10 per cent of their total output (see Table 7.8).

Table 7.8 Export potential of Brazilian computer firms

Export potential	Source of technology		
	Own	Licensing	Total
Good (more than 10% of total sales)	6	1	7 (30%)
Bad (less than 10% of total sales)	5	11	16 (70%)
Total	11	12	23 (100%)

The principal export market for Brazilian DP equipment was Latin America. Argentina, in particular, absorbed the first exports of Cobra which totalled US $1 million in 1980. Venezuela and Chile might also become importers of Brazilian computer products in the near future. Mexico, which is the second largest computer user in Latin America after Brazil, is now introducing import restrictions in order to develop its own computer industry. Cobra estimates that its total exports to Latin America could reach US $5 million in the fiscal year 1981/2.

Although the Latin America DP equipment is actually an almost exclusive market for American firms, Brazilian firms might have certain competitive advantages. These include the language used in blueprints and manuals, and import duty rebates through Lafta (Latin American Free Trade Association).

In addition to the Latin American market, Brazilian entrepreneurs saw some business opportunities in Africa and in socialist countries. But, in general, they relied on official government support to approach those markets. The largest export deal so far was privately negotiated with China by Polymax. The deal involved the supply of 1000 locally developed microcomputers worth more than US $10 million during 1981–2. It included a commitment to technical assistance and technology transfer, as China was interested in developing its own computer industry.

Most managers interviewed were not optimistic about the prospects of exporting to OECD countries. Five firms exhibited their products at the 1980 and 1981 Hanover Fair. One VDU manufacturer said that the only way to penetrate the highly competitive European market was to compete on price, as Brazilian DP equipment had no reputation there and firms could not provide direct local technical assistance. He argued that Brazilian-made VDUs could be competitive only if priced 30 per cent below existing products. In addition, new entrants would have to offer high commissions in order to attract good representatives. Under these conditions the sale of VDUs to Europe was not considered attractive.

The findings of this study revealed that the most important factors affecting Brazilian firms capacity to export computer products were price and ability to develop original products. Local firms were more likely to succeed by exporting special products rather than standard ones. One example was a football pools terminal developed in-house by Racimec. The product had no similar competitor in the international market and the firm had potential to export 70 per cent of production.

On the other hand, computer products manufactured locally under licence from foreign firms were unlikely to have export potential. This may be due to the following reasons: first, many licensing agreements included unwritten export prohibition to specific countries or a ban on all exports. Second, licensers could produce at lower costs than their licensees because of their larger output which provided economies of scale in R & D and manufacturing. Consequently, they could export at lower prices than their licensees. Third, most licensers had established a marketing network abroad and sometimes overseas manufacturing facilities also. In contrast, their Brazilian licensees had limited marketing experience abroad. Since they manufactured the same products, marketing was a decisive advantage of licensers.

The evidence showed a strong negative statistical correlation between licensing agreement and export success ($Q = -0.859$).

Exports from Brazilian manufacturing subsidiaries of large multinationals constitute a special case. Typically, their export performance is a function of the policy of the corporation as a whole determined at Corporate Headquarters. IBM's international manufacturing strategy, for example, is based on three elements: costs, including manufacturing, freight and taxation; corporate strategy defined by the Board of Administration based on strategic and political considerations; and the size of the local market. Manufacturing operations are independent from R & D and marketing activities. Each one of these activities is integrated by the firm internationally instead of locally.

Brazilian branches of IBM and Burroughs have produced a relatively high volume of exports in recent years. But a high proportion of the value of products exported was derived from previously imported goods.

About 70 per cent of Brazilian computer firms had poor export prospects. Many of them were too new to have developed export capabilities. At the time of this study they were still structuring their internal marketing operations, and some firms had not yet examined the export opportunities. Firms which already counted on marketing as a major competitive advantage had good export potential. Correlation between these two factors was found to be significant $(Q = 0.529)$.

Firms which supplied systems usually had better export performance than peripheral manufacturers. Peripheral equipment is usually supplied on an OEM basis. In order to export peripherals, manufacturers have either to incorporate them in computer systems produced locally for export or to sell directly to foreign system houses which would integrate the peripherals into a computer system. Thus, the export opportunities of peripheral manufacturers without strong links with either foreign 'system houses' or computer manufacturers were not good. Statistical correlation between product sector (system) and export potential was fairly high $(Q = 0.525)$.

8 TECHNOLOGY STRATEGIES OF BRAZILIAN COMPUTER FIRMS

This chapter will analyse the technology strategies of Brazilian computer firms. This includes evaluating firms' research and development policies; analysing the reasons for undertaking licensing agreements; the difficulties and opportunities for R & D; and evaluating the factors which affect the content of local components in locally manufactured data-processing equipment. This will be done by testing the hypotheses set up in Part One.

1 RESEARCH AND DEVELOPMENT STRATEGIES

In 1980 Brazilian DP equipment manufacturers spent 8.7 per cent of total sales on R & D activities (see Table 8.1). By contrast, American computer and peripheral firms R & D expenditure constituted only 6.1 per cent of total sales. Brazilian computer firms also spent more on R & D per employee ($4730) than their American counterparts ($3265) (see Table 8.2).

Brazilian firms are still establishing their product lines and frequent innovations and changes are introduced in the technology. Therefore, products contain a high proportion of scientific and engineering inputs and R & D costs account for a higher proportion of total outlay. Although the computer industry is relatively new in the USA, compared to Brazilian firms, American firms have reached a more mature stage characterized by mass production and mass distribution. Thus, the ratios of R & D expenditures to sales and R & D employees to total personnel have declined. The current stage of the Brazilian computer industry can be summarized by Hirsch's (1965) characteristics of the product cycle at the early stage (see Table 8.3).

Because computers are in an early stage of the product cycle, and because there was a 'market reserve' policy, which kept away competition from multinational firms, many firms relied exclusively on local technological sources to establish their product lines. The relative technological effort of such firms was greater than that of those which chose licensing as a path to acquire technology. In 1980

Table 8.1 Estimate of sales and research and development expenditure in the Brazilian computer industry, 1980

	Firm	Main product	R & D expenditure US $10³ [a]	Sales US $ 10³ [b]	R & D as per cent of sales
Licenses	Cobra	Minicomputers	10 966	131 600	8.3
	SID	Minicomputers	3483	38 280	9.1
	Labo	Minicomputers	1376	27 528	5.0
	Edisa	Minicomputers	1255	16 729	7.5
	Globus Digital	Printers and tape drives	1280	12 793	10.0
	Elebra Informatica	Printers and disk drives	900	10 825	8.3
	Microlab	Tape and disk drives	784	7841	10.0
	Coencisa	Modems	423	6530	6.5
	Digilab	Printers	144	5776	2.5
	Multidigit	Disk drives	140	4684	3.0
	Compart	Tape drives	n.a.	4605	n.a.
	Flexidisk	Floppy disk drive	317	3175	10.0
	Moddata	Modems	n.a.	2237	n.a.
	Sub-total		21 068	272 603[c] 265 761[d]	7.9
Own development	Sisco	Minicomputers	n.a.	12 990	n.a.
	Scopus	Terminals, microcomputers	1293	10 773	12.0
	Polymax	Microcomputers	1665	9250	18.0
	Prologica	Microcomputers	500	6314	7.9
	Medidata	Microcomputers	463	4920	9.4
	Dismac	Microcomputers	n.a.	4640	n.a.
	Digiponto	Electronic keyboards	n.a.	3200	n.a.
	Quartzil	Microcomputers	n.a.	1771	n.a.
	Hybrid	Electronic accounting machines	n.a.	1264	n.a.
	Exata	Electronic accounting machines	90	900	10.0
	Embracomp	Terminals	100	718	13.9
	Parks	Modems	n.a.	717	n.a.
	Digirede	Microcomputers	794	460	172.6
	Sub-total		4905	57 917	14.4
	Total		25 973	330 520[c] 299 813[d]	8.7
	American Computer Industry composite[e]		3 031 700	49 889 000	6.1

Note: Values in cruzeiros were converted into US dollars at the mid-1980 exchange rate of US $1 = Cr $50.81

[a] Source: Interviews.
[b] Source: Digibras (1981)—except when another source is indicated.
[c] Sub-total.
[d] Sub-total with information about R & D expenditure.
[e] Source: *Business Week*, 7 July 1980.

Table 8.2 Estimate of R & D and personnel employed in the Brazilian computer industry, 1980 (end of the year)

Firm	Personnel		$\frac{1}{2}$	R & D expenditure per employee US $
	1 R & D	2 Total		
Licensees				
Cobra	325	1921	16.9	5708
SID	70	700	10.0	4975
Labo	52	501	10.4	2746
Edisa	45	289	15.5	4342
Coencisa	10	218	4.6	1940
Microlab[a]	9	70	12.9	11 200
Globus	23	140	16.4	9142
Elebra Informatica	25	127	19.7	7087
Digilab	11	82	13.4	1756[b]
Moddata	8	53	15.1	n.a.
Flexidisk	4	38	10.5	8342
Compart	n.a.	41	n.a.	n.a.
Multidigit	2	10	20.0	n.a.
Sub-total	584	4190[c] 4096[d]	14.1	5144
Own development				
Scopus	75	416	18.0	3108
Sisco	60	420	14.3	n.a.
Prologica	60	191	31.4	2618
Dismac	29	419	6.9	n.a.
Polymax	36	233	15.4	7146
Cape	20	100	20.0	n.a.
Itautec	60	166	36.1	n.a.
Parks	n.a.	120	n.a.	n.a.
Digirede	12	20	60.0	39 700
Racimec	9	70	12.8	n.a.
Digiponto	8	50	16.0	n.a.
Embracomp	6	40	16.9	2500
Exata	4	20	20.0	4500
Medidata	n.a.	75	n.a.	6173
Others	n.a.	304	n.a.	n.a.
Sub-total	379	2644 (3) 1395 (4)	17.5	3516 4730
Total	963	6834 (3) 5491 (4)	15.3	4730
American Industry Composite				3265

Sources: Interviews and Digibras (1981).

[a]Data-processing equipment only.
[b]Digilab receives additional product development help from Fundacao Bradesco;
[c]Total;
[d]Total with information about R & D expenditure.

Table 8.3 Characteristics of the product cycle

Characteristics	Cycle phase		
	Early	Growth	Mature
Technology	Short runs Rapidly changing techniques Dependence on external economies	Mass-production methods gradually introduced Variations in techniques still frequent	Long-runs and stable technology Few innovations of importance
Capital intensity	Low	High, due to high obsolescence rate	High, due to large quantity of specialized equipment
Industry structure	Entry is know-how determined Numerous firms providing specialized services	Growing number of firms Many casualties and mergers Growing vertical integration	Financial resources critical for entry Number of firms declining
Critical human inputs	Scientific and engineering	Management	Unskilled and semi-skilled labour
Demand structure	Sellers' market Performance and price of substitutes determine buyers' expectations	Individual producers face growing price elasticity Intra-industry competition reduces prices Product information spreading	Buyers' market Information easily available

Source: Hirsch (1965).

their average R & D expenditure was 14.4 per cent of total sales compared to 7.9 per cent for the latter (see Table 8.1).

The Brazilian computer industry is not sufficiently mature to have evolved clear R & D strategies. Often, firms have adopted different strategies for each of their various product lines. These include development of completely new products (in the Brazilian context), development of products to compete with equipment already in the market, further development of products originally designed in Brazil and the adaptation of licensed products both to improve performance and to increase the content of local components. The R & D activities of Brazilian computer and peripheral manufactures are shown in Table 8.4.

Table 8.4 Research and development activities of Brazilian computer firms

R & D activity	Firms		
	Yes	No	Total
Development of completely new products	10	13	23
Development to compete with existing products	16	7	23
Further development of products designed in Brazil	14	9	23
Adaptation of licensed products for nationalization	11	1	12
Adaptation of licensed products improve performance	3	9	12

Source: Interviews.

The nature of these R & D activities does provide a basis for analysing Brazilian computer firms' design strategies. The framework of analysis is based on Freeman's (1974) classification of firm's strategies, but some modifications have been introduced in order to take account of the specific characteristics of the Brazilian computer industry.

Design strategies concern the type of R & D activity developed by the firm according to Table 8.4. Firms' size, source of technology, product sector, personnel employed in R & D and competitive advantages have been statistically related to design strategies. Table 8.5 shows the bivariate correlations (Yules' Q) between all those variables collapsed into dichotomous categories. The correlation coefficients were subjected to the chi-square test.

Table 8.5 Research and development and competitive advantages correlation matrix

	1 Size	2 Source of techn.	3 R & D develop new	4 R & D develop simil.	5 R & D further dev.	6 Prod. sector	7 R & D personnel	8 CA Mark	9 CA Fin. R.	10 CA Product	11 CA Tech.
1 Size	1	0.412	−0.543[a]	0.895[a]	−0.647[a]	0.273	−0.333	0.698[a]	0.280	−0.428	−0.176
2 Source of technology	0.412	1	−0.860[a]	−0.143	−0.454	−0.555[a]	−0.454	0.325	0.385	0.263	−0.058
3 R & D dev. complete new products	−0.543[a]	−0.860[a]	1	−0.379	0.647[a]	0.411	0.333	−0.698[a]	−0.698[a]	0.481	0.176
4 R & D dev. similar products	0.895[a]	−0.143	−0.379	1	0.111	0.818[a]	0.111	0.463	0.463	−0.565	−0.529[a]
5 R & D further development	−0.647[a]	−0.454	0.647[a]	0.111	1	−0.250	0.180	−0.655[a]	−0.294	−0.714[a]	0.636[a]
6 Product sector	0.273	−0.555[a]	0.411	0.818[a]	−0.250	1	0.111	0.803[a]	0.059	0.525[a]	−0.754[a]
7 R & D personnel	−0.333	−0.454	0.333	0.111	0.180	0.111	1	−0.630[a]	−0.294	0.111	1[a]
8 Comp. advantage—Marketing	0.698[a]	0.325	−0.698[a]	0.463	−0.655[a]	0.803[a]	−0.630[a]	1	0.647[a]	−0.091	−0.351
9 Comp. advantage—Financial resources	0.280	0.385	−0.698[a]	0.463	−0.294	0.059	−0.294	0.647[a]	1	−0.529[a]	−1[a]
10 Comp. advantage—Product design	−0.428	0.263	0.481	−0.565	−0.714[a]	0.525[a]	0.111	−0.091	−0.529[a]	1	−0.529[a]
11 Comp. advantage—Technical capabilities	−0.176	−0.058	0.176	−0.529[a]	0.636[a]	−0.754[a]	1[a]	−0.351	−1[a]	−0.529[a]	1

[a] Significant correlation.
Obs: Size: small/medium and large; source of technology: licensing/own development; Research and Development: completely new products (yes/no) development of similar products to those already in the market (yes/no), further development of products designed in Brazil (yes/no); product sectors: system/peripheral; R & D personnel: more than 15 per cent of total labour force/less than 15 per cent; competitive advantages: marketing (yes/no), financial resources (yes/no), product design (yes/no), technical capabilities (yes/no).

Size of firms, source of technology and production sector were already defined in the previous chapter. To obtain an understanding of R & D strategies differences another differentiation was made between firms which employed more than 15 per cent of their total labour force in R & D activities (14 firms) and those which employed less than 15 per cent in those activities (9 firms). Finally, the analysis examined four types of comparative competitive advantages which the firms considered themselves to enjoy. Of the 23 firms, 6 were strong in marketing, 6 in financial resources, 16 had a good product design, and 6 had technical strength as competitive advantage.

Development of completely new products—the innovative firm

Data-processing equipment is defined as 'new' when no other similar product is already being manufactured locally. A new product in the Brazilian market is not necessarily a new product in the international market. Thus, the 'development of completely new products' may also involve the emulation of models designed abroad. In fact, many data-processing products developed by Brazilian companies have been based on foreign models. Original developments are undertaken primarily when local customers demand specific products which are not available abroad. Development of new products should then be understood as an autonomous development of equipment not previously manufactured locally. The form 'new' may be inadequate to describe some imitative developments which are included in this category. However, it was utilized in the analysis as there is no term in the literature on innovation to satisfactorily describe this.

Typically innovative firms lacked other competitive advantages such as marketing and financial resources. A negative correlation was found between development of new products and these ($Q = -0.698$ for both). Such firms adopted the policy of being first to introduce new products and quickly exploit the possibilities offered by the market. In general they were technically oriented and enjoyed a special relationship with the local scientific community through the recruitment of key individuals. Even when firms' product lines are imitations of foreign models, strong technical strength is required. Local firms might not have access to the same components utilized in the original design due to the necessity of incorporating locally manufactured components. Also, some components utilized by large computer manufacturers might not be made available to

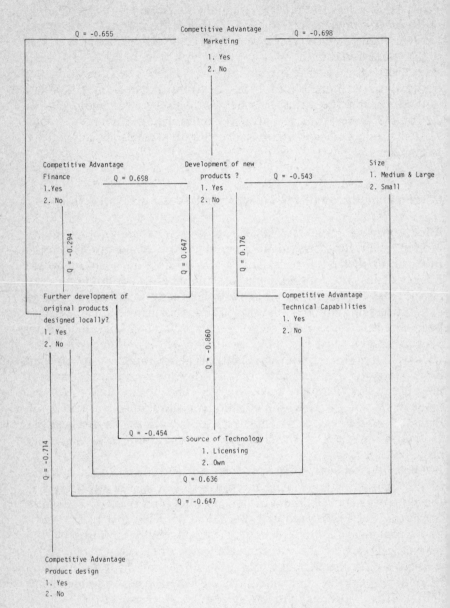

Fig. 8.1 Characteristics of the innovative firm

outsiders.[1] The imitation of a piece of data-processing equipment may thus require substantial modifications in original product design.

Innovators tended to be small firms. The negative correlation between size and the development of completely new products was $Q = -0.543$. In a study on the television industry, Sciberras (1979) suggested that little league firms tended to be the principal introducers of minor technical change. This also seems to occur in the Brazilian computer industry. Small firms tended to pursue a strategy of differentiating their product from the leaders' in order to secure a market share. The development of new products is also an entry strategy for many small firms which lack competitive advantages such as marketing and financial strength.

There is a highly negative correlation between source of technology (i.e. licensing or other sources) and development of new products $(Q = -0.860)$. This suggests that firms which enter into licensing agreements are seldom 'innovators'. Rather, it was mainly firms without licensing links which became involved in the development of new products. No evidence was found, however, that innovator firms employed a larger proportion of their personnel in R & D activities than non-innovator firms, since the correlation between those variables is not significant $(Q = -0.333)$.

Firms which developed completely new products tended also to undertake further development of products originally designed in Brazil, since the correlation between those two strategies is fairly high $(Q = 0.647)$. In fact, firms which adopted the latter design strategy are a special category of innovators. They have to be particularly strong in adaptive development in order to transform basic university designs into industrial products. Often, prototypes designed at universities and research centres make use of components and small-scale assembly processes which cannot be justified economically at larger scales of production. The manufacturing firm has thus to redesign products and also develop appropriate process designs and applications. Those firms have strong links with the local scientific community. Their major competitive advantage is technical capabilities $(Q = 0.636)$. But they lack other competitive advantages such as marketing and product design. Correlation between these and further development of products designed in Brazil is $Q = -0.655$ and $Q = -0.714$ respectively.

---

[1] IBM, for example, have exclusive access to specially designed microchips which are only manufactured in-house or exclusively produced by a sub-contractor.

Development of similar products—defensive or imitative firms

A large number of firms adopted 'defensive or imitative' strategies. This involves the development of products to compete with similar models already in the market. According to Freeman (1974) the main difference between defensive and imitative strategies is that the 'defensive' innovator does not normally aim to produce a carbon-copy imitation of the products introduced by early innovators. On the contrary, he hopes to take advantage of their early mistakes to improve upon their design, and he must have the technical strength to do so. On the other hand, the 'imitative' firm does not aspire to 'leap-frogging' or even 'keeping up with the game'. It is content to follow way behind the leaders in established technologies, often a long way behind.

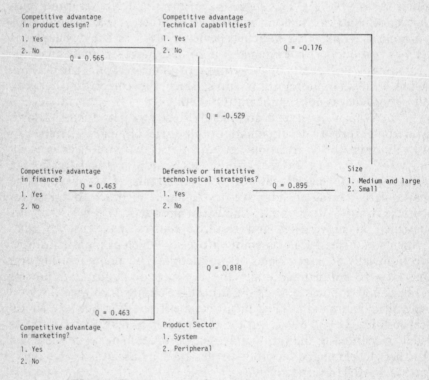

Fig. 8.2 Characteristics of the defensive or imitative firms

However, the differentiation between defensive and imitative strategies is not clear in the case of Brazilian computer industry. As the products are using the same components there is no technology lag. In this study these categories will be treated collectively, since they have many similar characteristics.

Part of the explanation for the non-existence of technology lags lies in the government policy towards standardization of data-processing equipment components with view to a future import substitution effort. The microcomputer manufacturer Novadata, for example, submitted to Capre a microcomputer design project based on a 16-bit microprocessor, Intel 8086. Since other manufacturers based their products on the 8-bit microprocessor, Intel 8085, Capre encouraged Novadata to do the same. Capre believed that the differentiation of component parts would jeopardize local semiconductor manufacturing plans as viability was dependent upon a minimum scale of operations. The same argument drove Capre to turn down Coencisa's 2400 bps digital modem manufacturing plans based on LSI integrated circuits. Capre believed that the product could adequately be based on MSI integrated circuits without increasing final production costs. The utilization of LSI i.c. in low-speed digital modems could force the market to reject MSI-based products which are already being manufactured in Brazil. According to Capre, this could have a double negative effect. First, the use of LSI in digital modems implies import costs nearly ten times higher than those of MSI. Second, the encouragement of widespread use of LSI could disrupt the plans of Brazilian manufacturers to start manufacturing MSI integrated circuits.

Defensive or imitative strategies involve both own product development and licensing. Firms within this category often rely on experimental development and design. But they do not rely on technical capabilities as much as innovators. This is suggested by the negative correlation between technical capabilities as a stated competitive advantage and defensive or imitative development ($Q = -0.529$).

Many firms combined 'defensive or imitative' with other design strategies in different segments of their product lines. Often firms adopted defensive designs to complete their product range. For example, most minicomputer manufacturers diversified towards the low-end segment of the computer market by developing less-powerful microcomputers and terminals which were already being manufactured locally by competitors. They relied on the advantages of having already established manufacturing and marketing facilities rather than on radical product change.

Minicomputer manufacturers enjoyed the advantage of having a captive market for VDUs, since mainframe computers usually require this kind of input/output device. Also, financial institutions which became involved in the computer industry, like Bradesco and Banco ITAU, had a large 'captive market' to support their development of bank terminals.

The vast majority of computer systems manufacturers adopted defensive or imitative development in at least one segment of their product range. Correlation between production sector (system and peripherals) and the development of products to compete with models already in the market was very high ($Q = 0.818$).

Sometimes, defensive or imitative firms enjoyed important cost advantages. These included incentive provided by the tax-free industrial state of Manaus; managerial efficiency which enabled lower overheads and training costs; access to technical information; and already established manufacturing facilities in electronics.

The statistical evidence shows that financially strong firms tended to adopt defensive or imitative design strategies ($Q = 0.463$). These firms had the financial resources to develop more applied software or provide better technical assistance for their customers than their predecessors did. They used a combination of product differentiation, technical services and good production engineering to secure a market share not attainable by product or technical innovations. A strong correlation was also found between size and defensive or imitative strategies ($Q = 0.895$). This strongly suggests that these strategies are pursued by large firms.

The dependent firm

Dependent firms are those which play a subordinate role in relation to their parents or licensers. The dependent firms' process and product engineering departments simply translate, interpret and detail the drawings and technical procedures received from their licensers or parents.

The clearest example of dependent strategies in the Brazilian computer industry is provided by manufacturing subsidiaries of multinational corporations. These firms make no effort to initiate technical changes in their product line locally without specific instructions from their parents. They may develop some applied software but seldom undertake hardware developments by themselves. If forced by high import taxes or direct government pressures to increase the content of components sourced locally, subsidiaries resort to local sub-contractors to duplicate components used by the company worldwide. Sometimes, even technologically simple parts, such as cables and screws, are considered more feasible to import because they are produced on a large scale by another subsidiary. Consequently, the content of local components in data-processing equipment manufactured in Brazil by subsidiaries of multinational corporations is typically lower than in equipment produced by locally owned firms. Even though IBM is making an effort to double the content of local components of the 4300 line, in 1983 only 20 per cent will be locally sourced.

Some Brazilian DP equipment manufacturers are pursuing a dependent strategy in at least one segment of their product line. Typically, these firms are much smaller than their licensers and lack the technical capability autonomously to develop products. In theory, dependent firms may enjoy the security of manufacturing established products. However, in practice, bankruptcies and take-overs may be common since the firms are vulnerable to the changes of licensers' attitude towards the sale of technology. Non-price competition based on inflow of innovations characterizes the computer market. Dependent firms' survival therefore requires access to innovation provided by their suppliers. But such dependence upon suppliers' technology means that these firms never develop their own capabilities. They are trapped in a vicious circle of dependence.

The main difference between a local manufacturing subsidiary of an MNC and a locally owned dependent firm is that the former is an overseas department of a resourceful and technically sophisticated large firm, while the latter retains a formal independence but has less access to financial and managerial resources.

Table 8.6 summarizes the characteristics of the Brazilian computer industry technology strategies.

2   FACTORS IN THE DECISION FOR TECHNOLOGY LICENSING

Licensing was the most common means of obtaining technology for a number of data-processing products (see Table 8.7). For magnetic disk drives, tape drives and high-speed modems (2400 bytes per second or more), all the equipment manufactured in Brazil was licensed. For minicomputers, printers and floppy-disk drives there was some local design, but licensed products held most of the market. At the time of this study, printers and floppy disk drives were being developed locally but had not yet reached the market. Only in mini-computers, where the principal technology is often embodied in the

Table 8.6 Characteristics of technology strategies

Technology strategy	Source of technology	Competitive advantages	Typical firm size	Relationship with local scientific community
Innovative	Own development	Technical strength	Small	Close
Defensive and imitative	Own development and licensing	Adaptative development: Marketing and Financial strength	Large	Intermittent
Dependent	Licensing	Product design Brand name	–	Distant

microelectronic component, were there locally designed products in direct competition with licensed equipment.

Table 8.8 summarizes the reasons given by Brazilian computer and peripheral manufacturers for acquiring technology through licensing. Each manager interviewed was asked to indicate factors which had a major influence over his decision to enter into license agreements for each product line manufactured under license.

Attitude of competitors and time required for local product development

The major reason given for licensing was competition. This had a decisive influence in nine licensing agreements which represents 60 per cent of the agreements referred to. Firms claimed that they entered licensing agreements because competitors did so or because the time required for in-house product development was too long.

The risks associated with late entry are particularly high in the computer peripheral business. The incorporation of a peripheral into a computer system requires the development of interfaces and the addition of support software to make the peripheral usable with the computer. Since peripherals are usually supplied on an OEM basis, computer manufacturers have to establish their own final assembly and testing procedures. The time and investment required for this do not encourage unnecessarily frequent changes in the type of peripheral used in a computer system. In 1979 most recently established minicomputer manufacturers in Brazil bought their peripheral equipment from OEM suppliers. Thus, peripheral manufacturers which already had marketable products and established reputations had an important competitive advantage over late market entrants.

Design and development is risky. Local firms had little incentive

Table 8.7 Source of technology by product line

Product	Source of technology		Total
	License	Other	
Microcomputers	—	11 (100%)	11 (100%)
Electronic accounting machines	—	7 (100%)	7 (100%)
Mini and mid-range computers	5 (71%)	2 (29%)	7 (100%)
Terminals (including intellig.)	—	5 (100%)	5 (100%)
Bank terminals	—	10 (100%)	10 (100%)
Data entry	—	4 (100%)	4 (100%)
Printers	3 (75%)	1 (25%)	4 (100%)
Magnetic disk drives	3 (100%)	—	3 (100%)
Floppy disk drives	3 (60%)	2 (40%)	5 (100%)
Magnetic tape drives	3 (100%)	—	3 (100%)
Keyboards	—	1 (100%)	1 (100%)
Modems—high speed	3 (100%)	—	3 (100%)
Modems—low speed	—	6 (100%)	6 (100%)
Word processor	—	2 (100%)	2 (100%)
Cartridge tape drives	—	1 (100%)	1 (100%)
Total	20 (28%)	52 (72%)	72 (100%)

Note: Projects approved by Capre/SEI.

Table 8.8 Reasons given for acquiring technology through licensing

	Product line					Total	% of total licensing agreements
	Disk drive (hard and floppy)	Tape drive	Printer	Modem	Mini-computer		
Attitude of competitors or time required by local development	3	2	1	1	1	9	60
Complexity of the technology	1	2	2	—	1	6	40
Risk of undertaking product development	2	—	1	—	1	4	27
Brand name and previous relationship with licenser ·	1	—	1	1	1	4	27
Cost advantages	1	—	—	—	1	2	13

Note: Complexity of technology includes both product and process design.
The interviews covered 10 firms and involved IS licensing agreements which represents 75 per cent of the total indicated in Table 8.8.
Firms were allowed to give one or more reasons for undertaking licensing.

to undertake it when they faced direct competition with licensed products which were proven and enjoyed goodwill. This could not be matched by locally designed products without years of proven success.

The example of disk-drive manufacturers Multidigit is a good illustration of this. The firm's initial plan was to design and develop their own product line in-house. One associated firm already had an R & D team which acquired experience by developing other data-processing equipment. A Brazilian engineer who worked as R & D manager for an American disk-drive manufacturer had agreed to lead the team. The product was to be based on similar models and developed over a period of between 20 and 24 months. However, two other disk-drive manufacturing projects based on licensed techno-logy were approved by Capre, on the grounds that the local market needed to be supplied promptly. This forced Multidigit to enter into licensing negotiations with an American disk-drive manufacturer. There was some scepticism about the competitive strength of locally designed products in a market where standards had been set by foreign technology. Thus product development would be undertaken by Multidigit only if competitors did the same.

A similar problem arose with the recently developed 'Winchester technology' for floppy-disk drives. Four firms submitted plans to the SEI to manufacture Winchester disk drives in Brazil. They were Micro-lab, Elebras, Multidigit and Flexidisk. While the first three firms would undertake their own product development, the fourth would acquire the product design from Shugart which was already supplying Flexi-disk with floppy-disk technology. But the three firms made it clear that, if SEI authorized the Flexidisk deal with Shugart, they would give up developing the Winchester technology in Brazil, and would also enter into licensing agreements to obtain the technology (*Datanews*, 17 December 1980). In June 1981 SEI decided not to authorize licensing agreements for the Winchester technology and to give local firms a two-year period to develop the floppy disk in-house.

The findings of this study suggest that pressure of competition may be a more important reason for entering into licensing agree-ments than the difficulty of understanding and developing the technology itself. This lends support to the hypothesis (Hyp. 4.2) that licensing is made necessary by the competitive environment.

Complexity of the technology

The lack of technical ability to develop product or process design in-house was the second most cited reason for entering into licensing agreements. Six agreements, representing 40 per cent of the sample, were directly influenced by this factor. Two-thirds of the agreements involved either printer or tape-drive technology. The high concentration in these two products may be a result of the high-precision mechanical technology required for their development and manufacture, where there are very few skilled professionals available locally.

One firm could have asked a local university to design and develop a tape-drive model, but it needed technical support to develop the manufacturing of some key components and this could not be arranged locally. It therefore felt compelled to acquire a complete technology package from an experienced foreign manufacturer.

The hypothesis (Hyp. 4.1) states that licensing is made necessary by the complexity of technology. In the Brazilian computer industry this appears to be valid for a number of products. But in others like modems, minicomputers and disk drives, lack of technological skills only play a secondary role in firms' decisions to acquire technology through licensing.

Risks of undertaking product development in-house and cost advantages

Risks of undertaking product development in-house include uncertainties about price, quality standards and market conditions. Firms minimize some of these risks when they gain access to an already tested technology through licensing agreements.

In the first year of operations, licensing agreements involve the import of fully assembled products on a monopoly basis. Products usually begin to be assembled locally in the second year. One of the main advantages of this process is that licensees can develop the market before starting the manufacturing phase. They can develop expertise in marketing, technical assistance and management before facing the additional risks involved in manufacturing and product development operations. Four licensing agreements, representing 27 per cent of the total, were found to have been influenced principally by this factor.

Cost advantage was the least-cited reason for undertaking license agreements. Only two firms felt that the relatively lower cost of licensing as compared to own product development was a major driving force in their decision on technology sourcing.

The findings of this study reveal that risks avoidance or minimization are more important than costs benefits in the decision of acquiring technology through licensing. The findings give limited support

to the hypothesis (Hyp. 4.3) that licensing is made necessary by the
cost advantages and to the risk of own product development.

Brand name and previous relationship with licensers

'Brand name' considerations were not found to be a strong reason
for licensing. In the Brazilian computer industry licensing agreements
did not include the use of licensers' brand names. In only two instances
did licensees maintain that the goodwill enjoyed by the licensers was
a major reason for licensing. In two others, licensees admitted that
their previous partnerships with licensers was the principal reason
for the agreement.

These findings did not tend to support the hypothesis (Hyp. 4.4)
that licensing is made necessary by the advantages of gaining access
to particular brand names and by previous relationships with licensers.

3   DIFFICULTIES AND OPPORTUNITIES OF RESEARCH AND DEVELOPMENT ACTIVITIES IN THE BRAZILIAN COMPUTER INDUSTRY

Three factors were identified as having a major influence over the
R & D policies of Brazilian computer firms. They are the availability
of high-level engineers and technicians,[2] the extent of technology
flow from abroad and government support—both financial and
institutional—through the establishment of non-tariff barriers.
Table 8.9 summarizes the opinions of firms in the industry concerning factors affecting their R & D activities.

Availability of high-level engineers and technicians

From 1975 to 1980 the number of Brazilian DP equipment manufacturers grew twelvefold—from 4 to 50. This had a massive impact
on the demand for highly qualified R & D professionals. In 1980 the
23 major Brazilian DP equipment manufacturers employed around
1000 people in R & D activities (see Table 8.2).

The existing electronics, electrical and communications industries
provided most of the quality control and process technology personnel required by the new DP industry. Since 1978 some segments of
the communications industry have faced a sharp decline in sales,
due to cuts in government expenditure. Consequently, they made
redundant many of their engineers and technicians. These were

[2] In Brazil the formation of engineers involves 4 to 5 years' of university training.
Technicians usually undertake 3 years' of secondary courses.

Table 8.9 Difficulties and opportunities for R & D in the Brazilian computer industry

Factors affecting R & D activities	Firms' main technological source		
	Licensing	Own	Total
Supply of high-level technologists			
Good	4	–	4 (25%)
Bad (lack experience, few professionals available)	4	8	12 (75%)
Availability of licensing agreements			
Plays a positive role	7	2	9 (82%)
Plays a negative role	–	2	2 (18%)
Government support			
(a) Financial support			
Good	1	1	2 (13%)
Weak (few resources, bureaucracy)	3	4	7 (47%)
None	4	2	6 (40%)
(b) 'Market reserve' policy			
Plays a positive role	7	7	14 (100%)
Plays a negative role	–	–	–

absorbed by the computer industry. Most of Cobra's quality-control engineers, for example, originated from Standard Electric.

However, the new computer industry demanded a larger number of highly trained professionals who were not currently available in the local labour market. The foreign firms which supplied the Brazilian computer market trained local engineers and technicians to perform customers' support activities and to develop some application software. Since they did not operate R & D activities in Brazil, they were unable to train professional manpower to perform those activities.

In particular, the new computer industry faced problems in recruiting engineers experienced in systems software[3] and hardware design and development. The main source of such skilled manpower in Brazil was the post-graduate programmes and university research centres in computer science. But engineers coming directly from the university were generally prepared for basic research and lacked experience in industrial development environment requirements. Consequently, many professionals had to be sent abroad by the local firms to attend appropriate industrial courses and to be trained by technology suppliers.

[3] System software serves two major purposes: it aids the development of system and applications software, and it controls the execution of software in the computer.

Although most major Brazilian computer and peripherals manufacturers completed the establishment of their R & D teams by the
end of 1979, 75 per cent of the managers interviewed reported
problems concerning highly skilled engineers and technicians. Firms
said that salaries were inflated and that there was an excessive
mobility of professionals in the industry. Minicomputer manufacturers were particularly worried about the high turnover of
qualified personnel. In 1980 they had a first meeting to discuss
the subject and propose a code of practice to prevent 'head hunting'
between them. Firms also started to implement industrial relations
policies designed to prevent defection of engineers to competitors.

University centres provided additional help on product design to
many firms. Edisa, for example, contracted part of the development
of its data-entry equipment to the Federal University of Rio Grande
do Sul. This included the external design and a small-scale supply of
circuit boards. Also Cobra, Embracomp, Globus and Microlab among
others have contracts with universities for the development of new
products.

Another source of R & D help was Brazilian and foreign independent
computer designers. Racimec, for example, designed in-house a
cassette tape-drive unit by contracting out its development to two
independent American engineers.

The availability of skilled engineers seems to vary from region
to region. Firms located in São Paulo, where more than 50 per cent
of the Brazilian DP industry is located, were particularly affected
by the shortage of such skills. All firms interviewed in that region
reported a shortage of highly qualified R & D personnel. But other
manufacturing centres like Porto Alegre and Brasília seemed to have
no problems in finding R & D personnel (See Table 8.10). A possible
reason for this is that these cities have a relatively small demand for
R & D personnel which are promptly attended by local universities.

The shortage of high-level engineers seems not to constitute a
major obstacle to the development of R & D activities in the Brazilian
computer industry. It may have encouraged firms' decisions to
undertake licensing agreements. However, in many cases, this influence was seen as secondary rather than central.

Availability of licensing agreements

There are two views concerning the influence of licensing agreements
over the development of local technology. The first view is that
technology acquired through licensing agreements competes with
local technology developments. Thus licensing is seen as inhibiting

Table 8.10 Regional availability of high-level engineers

Firms' location	Supply of high-level technologists		
	Good	Bad[a]	Total
São Paulo	–	8	8
Rio de Janeiro	1	4	5
Rio Grande do Sul	2	–	2
Brasilia	1	–	1
Total	4	12	16

[a]Supply of high-level technologists was qualified as 'bad' when firms reported having problems such as lack of experience and few professionals available.

the development of local capabilities through capturing a market that could otherwise be supplied by local technological sources.

The second view is that licensing agreements help the development of local technological capabilities. This view is supported by over 80 per cent of the firms interviewed, including two firms which did not undertake any licensing agreements. In general, firms tended to share the opinion that foreign technology was a short cut for the latest technology. Licences substantially reduced the time required to start up local production of data-processing equipment and helped to avoid mistakes both in product and process design that would be inevitable with reliance exclusively on local technological sources.

One technical director interviewed found that licensing played a positive role only when the licensed firm had the necessary capability to learn the technology and to request further information from licensers. Also, the licensed firm must be skilled enough to adapt foreign process and product design to local market conditions.

Two firms shared the opinion that giving contracts to high-level foreign engineers, either as consultants or employees, may sometimes be cheaper and more appropriate for the firm than licensing agreements.

Government financial support

At the time of this study the level and quantity of government financial support for the computer industry did not seem to be matching firms' requirements. Only two firms (13 per cent) interviewed said they were receiving appropriate financial support from official institutions. Seven firms (47 per cent) complained about excessive bureaucracy when obtaining government credits for R & D and about the scarcity of the resources allocated to those operations. Three of them said that guarantees required by the official institutions to release credit was as tight as those required by private banks. Six firms (40 per cent) said that they had no access to official credits so far.

Private financial institutions are investing more in the Brazilian computer industry than official institutions. Some commercial banks like Bradesco, Itau and Iochpe are major shareholders of computer-manufacturing firms while many other private banks hold a minor partnership.

Weak official financial support for the computer sector may curb the development of local technology. Private capital is primarily concerned with security returns on profit maximization often in the short term. Risky R & D programmes are not an attractive proposition for such investors. Pure financial cost-benefit analysis may encourage Brazilian firms to undertake licensing agreements rather than their own research. Many firms made the development of some risky projects conditional upon obtaining subsidized credits from official institutions. One example is the mid-range DEC-compatible computer designed by NCE/UFRJ. Edisa, which currently manufacture a minicomputer model under license from Fujitsu, had already signed a contract with NCE/UFRJ to develop, manufacture and market the new mid-range computer. But in view of the high investment required, and the uncertainty presented by the project, Edisa decided to wait for official financial support before adopting an autonomous path in mainframe computers.

Some recent steps undertaken by the government, however, may bring further financial resources to the industry. This includes government direct investment in Cobra and the opening of a credit line through Finame for financing the sale of Brazilian DP equipment.

The influence of market reserve policy on research and development activities

The protectionist policy established at the end of 1977 for the computer industry was unanimously backed by Brazilian firms. Most managers interviewed believed that an indigenous computer industry would not exist if they had to compete directly with large multinational corporations. They also believed that foreign licensers would have preferred to set up wholly owned manufacturing subsidiaries in Brazil if this were accepted by the government. Consequently, local firms would not have had access to foreign technology. The attitudes of Brazilian computer industry entrepreneurs clearly supports the hypothesis (Hyp. 1.2) that direct investment by multinational firms in developing countries restrains competition and imposes oligopolistic barriers to entry for indigenous firms.

The vast majority of firms wanted the policy to be continued for a long time. They said that they made substantial investments in technology which would not be profitable under direct competition with multinationals. Some entrepreneurs were worried about the institutional changes which occurred at the beginning of 1980 in the computer industry. They feared that the new state agency which took over Capre's responsibility might adopt a more liberal policy towards foreign direct investment.

Two or three firms argued that protection should be concentrated on technology rather than on the market. According to them, firms which developed their own products should have more incentives than those which simply acquired foreign technology through licensing agreements.

The effects of foreign competition, either through imports or through the setting up of local manufacturing capabilities, on the development of indigenous technology can be well illustrated by the Argentinian case. One director interviewed said that there was an integrated-circuit manufacturer—FAT—which started to develop and manufacture minicomputers. In 1976 the military junta which took over the government liberalized both imports and local manufacturing by foreign firms. Consequently, the financial group which backed FAT was discouraged from continuing to invest and the plans were discontinued. The high-level technical group involved in the minicomputer project was dispersed. Argentina now imports its computer needs.

4 LOCAL COMPONENTS CONTENT

The development of computers can be attributed, to a large extent, to the rapid and continuous process of technical change in electronics components. Some of the functions which were originally performed by the computer system through software design are now programmed into component hardware. Microprocessors can now incorporate many logic and control functions required by a minicomputer in a single chip. Consequently technical competitiveness in computers is becoming increasingly based upon the integration of computer component design and manufacturing.

Brazil has very limited capabilities in terms of several critical computer and peripheral components. This includes some high-precision mechanical components and microelectronic components.

High-precision mechanical components are widely utilized in computer peripheral equipment such as printers and magnetic storage equipments. Examples of precision components are hammer mechanisms of printers, stepping motors, and read/write heads of disk systems. Most require extreme accuracy in dimensions, forms and in tolerance of physical and chemical parameters. Some efforts have been made to manufacture some precise mechanisms of peripheral equipment in Brazil,[4] but there is little experience in the industry and a crucial shortage of highly skilled mechanical engineers.

For electronic components the problem is even more difficult. The manufacture of integrated circuits is a major strain on local capabilities, involving as it does very advanced product and process technology.

In Brazil there is local production of some discrete devices and of some types of integrated circuits. But this is oriented towards the consumer electronic market, rather than to the professional which has different, often higher technological requirements. In 1979 data processing represented only 13 per cent of the total electronic market in Brazil. In 1981 there were 13 semiconductor manufacturers in Brazil, of which only one was nationally owned. Foreign-owned semiconductor manufacturers did not have the diffusion stage of fabrication in Brazil. The vast majority of firms only assemble imported chips. Transit, the sole Brazilian semiconductor manufacturer, had a more integrated production. But due to financial and technical problems, the firm closed down its operations in 1981.

The semiconductor market for data-processing equipment in Brazil consists of many different types of components. This is exacerbated by the existence of several sources of technology; including 16 licensing agreements from five different countries. Consequently, the volume of sales of each type of component is not large enough to make local production economically viable.

At the time of this study, SEI was at the early stages of preparing a plan to standardize some components utilized locally. Under the proposed plan the government would specify a preferential list of components and encourage computer manufacturers through fiscal

---

[4] In 1980 Abramo Eberle Steel, which control printer manufacturer Digilab, established a subsidiary to manufacture high-precision mechanical components such as fan and stepping motors. Also, a special commission was created by SEI with representation from the private sector, universities and other governmental institutions to establish a development plan for the Brazilian high-precision mechanical industry.

and tariff mechanism to purchase them. The preferential list making different types of components uniform, will enable local production to operate on a more economical basis.

In April 1981 the government concluded an ambitious 'National Plan for Microelectronics'. The plan included the setting up of a Research Centre in microelectronics in Campinas, with an annual budget of $10 million; the acquisition of semiconductor technology from European firms (the leading American manufacturers refused to sell technology under the required conditions); and the establishment of 'market reserve' for two private Brazilian industrial groups to establish the manufacture of electronic components. In mid 1981 two companies were selected: Investimento Itau SA and Docas de Santos. Both companies are large private Brazilian business institutions and are already in the computer industry.

The semiconductor market is made up of discrete devices, integrated circuits and opto electronic devices. The 1980 value of the Brazilian market was estimated as US $180 million. The major discrete devices are transistors, diodes and rectifiers. The total market for discrete devices in Brazil in 1980 was $100 million, while the value of integrated circuits, both digital and linear, was $80 million. Digital integrated circuits are expected to dominate the semiconductor market by 1990 (see Table 8.11).

Table 8.11 Perspectives for the Brazilian Electronic market, 1980–90 US $1 000 000

Electronic component	1980	1985	1990	% growth 1980-90	% annual geometric growth
Discrete components	100	155	240	140	10.2
Linear integrated circuits	38	70	80	110	8.6
Digital integrated circuits	42	110	260	520	22.4
Total	180	335	580	220	13.9

Source: Comissao de Microelectronica SEI.

The components issue raised contradictions for policy which are not easily resolved given the state of development of the Brazilian computer industry.

On the one hand, to have an effective technology strategy for computers, requires some control over the design and manufacture of components. The world-leader computer manufacturers increasingly rely on in-house supply of main components. This includes in-house production of microprocessor units. Vertical integration brings cost advantages, control over quality of components and enables firms to effectively incorporate new technical development in components in computer products. A high degree of dependence on foreign supply of components can inhibit the future development of the local industry. If Brazil does not develop semiconductor design and production capability the local computer industry would have little control over supply and costs or the major computer hardware component and would be reduced to a passive role with respect to technical change. This can constrain the long-term competitiveness of local computer products.

On the other hand, the establishment of a local semiconductor industry is a very costly and risky venture. Even if the government contributed a high proportion of the required investment in R & D and manufacturing facilities, the quality, reliability and performance of the locally manufactured integrated circuit are unlikely immediately to match that of the imported components. Consequently, the competitiveness of the local computer industry might be impaired in the short term.

Computer products designed locally usually contained a higher proportion of local components than those produced under licence. In 1981, the locally designed computer Cobra 530 utilized 92 per cent of locally sourced components against only 80 per cent for minicomputers manufactured under licence. Consequently, firms which had acquired technology through licensing were more worried about product nationalization[5] programmes than those which had developed their own product lines. Two firms argued that the mere substitution of local for imported components was not feasible, since it involved a high redesigning cost. It was considered that extensive product nationalization efforts must be accompanied by an effort to improve the imported designs. Consequently, the final result of the redesign work would be not only the utilization of locally manufactured components but also the obtention of an improved product design.

The efforts of minicomputer makers to increase the content of local components of products manufactured under licence can well be illustrated by the case of Labo Electronica. Figure 8.3 shows the evolution of the 'nationalization level' of System 8034 produced under licence from the West German firm Nixdorf. Until December 1980 only tests were done in Brazil. In 1981 the equipment was imported as a semi-knocked down (SKD) form, but only the cabinet

---

[5] 'Product nationalization' refers to the content of nationally manufactured components in a final product manufactured in Brazil.

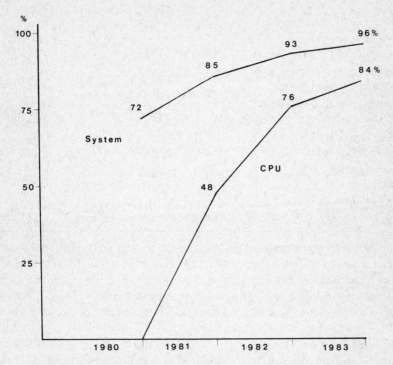

Fig. 8.3 Evolution of the nationalization level of Labo 8034

and peripherals were acquired locally. The third phase called 'completely knocked down' (CKD), was due to start by the end of 1981. It consists of importing only those components which were not available in the local market. In this phase the cost of imported components in the Central Processing Unit (CPU) was expected to drop from the original $25 000 to $4000 per unit.

Factors which affect firms' product nationalization programmes

Firms were asked to identify factors which played a positive, negative or neutral role in the efforts to increase the content of local components in their product lines. This is summarized in Table 8.12.

Import quotas for components

Strict governmental control over the import of components is by far the dominant factor inducing Brazilian data-processing equipment

Table 8.12 Factors which affect firm's product nationalization programmes

Factor	Positive role	Vary/ neutral	Negative role	Total
Import quotas for components	11 (92%)	1 (8%)	–	12 (100%)
Comparative cost advantages of local component supply	–	3 (38%)	5 (62%)	8 (100%)
Response of local component manufacturers	3 (25%)	4 (33%)	5 (42%)	12 (100%)
Quality and reliability of local components	2 (20%)	4 (40%)	4 (40%)	10 (100%)
In-house capacity to verticalize	6 (50%)	–	6 (50%)	12 (100%)
Speed of technical innovation in DP industry	1 (12%)	3 (38%)	4 (50%)	8 (100%)

manufacturers to increase the content of locally manufactured parts of their product lines. More than 90 per cent of firms affected by import control considered that it was the driving force behind their product nationalization programmes. Import restrictions affected firms in three ways. First, individual firms were allocated a fixed annual quota for imports. Any increase of output above a certain level would depend on a relative increase in the use of locally manufactured components. For example, if the content of imported components in a certain product is 20 per cent of the total cost, the maximum limit of production of this product would be five times the value of imports. Sales above this limit would be possible only if the nationalization level of the product were increased. Second, the allowance of import quotas depends on the minimum content of locally manufactured components contained in each product line. A minimum level of nationalization is established by the government for each kind of equipment on the basis of comparison between competitors. In 1978, for example, three projects for manufacturing electronic accounting machines were submitted to Capre. One firm —Exata—presented a locally designed model which required only $260 imported components per unit. The two other firms presented products developed abroad with a substantially higher content of imported components. In view of Exata's ability to intensively utilize local components, Capre asked the competitors to reduce their import requirements to a similar level as a condition for allowing an import quota. As a result, the two firms redesigned their models to reach a product nationalization level similar to that of

Exata. Third, the importation of components involves bureaucratic problems which may be costly and time consuming. Also, import duties have increased steadily in Brazil, with the worsening of the national balance of payments. From 1979 to 1980 import taxes for some computer components rose from 10 to 85 per cent, having an enormous impact on firms' cost and pricing.

Table 8.13 outlines the import quotas permitted in 1980 for major data-processing equipment manufacturers. The two foreign companies with manufacturing facilities at the time had a quota of $82 170 000; representing 57.25 per cent of the total quota $53 885 000 was for components for products to be exported and $28 285 000 was for products to be sold in the Brazilian market. Manufacturers of some peripheral equipment such as printers, tape drives and disk drives had a relatively high quota, as the content of locally manufactured components of these products was still very low at this time. Many firms were allowed a small quota (ranging from $5000 to $1 000 000) for product development. This enables the importation of components and capital goods to build a small number of prototype units. After completing product development, these firms usually apply for a larger import quota to enable production on an industrial scale.

Comparative costs of local components supply

The price of locally manufactured components did not encourage the efforts towards product nationalization. More than 60 per cent of the firms interviewed stated that, in general, locally manufactured components were more expensive than imported ones, while the others argued that some components were cheaper and some more expensive in Brazil than imported from abroad. However, the costs of imported components have been rising very fast as a result of increases in direct import duties and on taxes for acquiring foreign currency.[6]

Responsiveness of local component manufacturers

The responsiveness of Brazilian components suppliers to the needs of the local computer industry seems to vary. In general, the suppliers responsiveness to firms depended on the scale of the orders. They made efforts to meet the computer industry's technical and price requirements only when the value of orders was large enough to cover the additional cost of manufacturing specially designed components.

In advanced industrial countries electronic components manufacturers usually push the downstream industries towards technical

[6] In January 1981 the IOF (Imposto sobre Operacões Financeiras), a tax to be paid when buying foreign currencies, rose from 15 to 25 per cent.

Table 8.13 Import quotas allowed in 1980 (US $1000)

Firm	Import quota	% of total
IBM	74 547	51.94
internal market	(25 527)	(17.78)
for export	(49 020)	(34.16)
Cobra	26 638	18.56
Burroughs	7623	5.31
internal market	(2758)	(1.92)
for export	(4865)	(3.39)
Elebra Informatica	6470	4.51
Globus	4914	3.42
Multidigit	2906	2.04
Microlab	2460	1.71
Polymax	1900	1.32
Scopus	1809	1.26
Sisco	1613	1.12
SID	1398	0.97
Digilab	1290	0.89
Sharp	1084	0.75
Tecla	1083	0.75
Elebra Electronica	864	0.60
Exata	714	0.50
Edisa	658	0.46
Sisbra	609	0.42
Racimec	551	0.38
OZ Electronica	545	0.38
Embracomp	489	0.34
Prologica	466	0.32
Flexidisk	417	0.29
Zanthus	352	0.25
Gepeto	322	0.22
Dismac	304	0.21
Digiponto	230	0.16
MDA	202	0.14
Capre	178	0.12
Coencisa	170	0.12
Others[a]	1067	0.74
Total	143 513	100.00

Source: Capre.

[a]There were 19 other firms with import quotas under $150 000.

change. The development of the 256 KB microchip by American and Japanese semiconductor manufacturers for example, is driving the minicomputer manufacturers in these countries to increase the memory capacity of their products.

In Brazil, however, component manufacturers play a responsive role rather than an aggressive role, because they have a lower level of technological sophistication than computer manufacturers. The computer industry is more likely to influence suppliers to introduce technical change.[7]

One computer firm found that suppliers were not willing to invest in new products. The firm was compelled to undertake major efforts to adapt their own products to use the limited variety of local supply of components. The firm claimed that when a product is developed in the USA a wide range of components is available. Often the development team have several options of component dimensions and specifications. In Brazil, however, the local supply of components is much narrowed, making it more difficult to develop a competitive product.

Quality and reliability of locally manufactured components

Unfortunately, the findings regarding the extent to which quality and reliability of locally manufactured components affects computer firms' nationalization efforts is unclear. Forty per cent of the firms interviewed said that the quality varied according to the manufacturer and to the type of component. They argued that there was no 'national standard' for electronic components. In general, they were happy about the quality of discrete devices, but complained about the quality of other components. Another 40 per cent said that there was a general quality problem in components manufactured locally. One firm reported that the technological level of most suppliers was low. Another firm said that they had to give up utilizing some locally manufactured components because of quality problems. Finally, 20 per cent of the firms interviewed stated that the quality of local components was good, and that there was no difference in quality standards between local and imported components.

[7] The process of import-substitution, which has been the model for Brazilian industrialization process, usually, works as follows: First the product is locally assembled using imported components. Then the process of product nationalization begins. It involves the progressive implementation of local components production. Biondi (1975) called this process an 'upside down industrialization'.

In-house capacity to vertical integration

At the time of this study the level of vertical integration of the Brazilian computer industry was low. Ownership links between system and peripheral manufacturers were almost non-existent and, in the vast majority of cases, electronic-component manufacturers were not involved in the production of data-processing equipment.

Half of the firms interviewed said that they had both the technical and financial capacity to undertake in-house production of some important inputs. Three computer manufacturers said that they were likely to move into the market of peripheral equipment attached to their mainframe computers. Most minicomputer manufacturers have already developed terminals and data-entry systems. One firm felt compelled to move into the cassette tape drive market to assure a competitive price for the system which incorporates it. A printer maker started a new venture to produce key components which were not available in the local market. Finally, electronic firms which moved into the data-processing business also managed to manufacture some components in-house.

Vertical integration may become a very important competitive element in the near future. The capacity of firms to produce in-house peripherals and components can produce cost reductions. Price competitiveness is likely to become a major element for Brazilian computer firms' survival when the industry reaches a more mature stage. It also may enable a regular supply of components of required quality and reliability.

Speed of technical innovation in the data-processing industry

Computers have a short life cycle. This can have a negative impact on local manufacturers' plans to increase the content of locally manufactured components. Before being able to complete the 'nationalization' of a certain product, the firm may have to introduce a radical product change in order to keep up with competitors. Product change in the computer industry is usually motivated by the development of better components such as semiconductors. Since local component manufacturers have a passive rather than aggressive role, major product change usually involves the increase of the content of components which are not available locally and thus have to be imported. Subordinate licensees are especially vulnerable to this problem.

Half of the firms interviewed confirmed that product change had a negative role on their product nationalization programmes. About one-third found that product change did not have a discernible positive or negative influence. Only one firm said that product change has a positive impact on the increase of the nationalization level of its product lines.

Conclusion

The main reason for local component sourcing by Brazilian firms is government policies. Firms are primarily concerned with two critical competitive elements: cost and performance of their equipment. In the short term, the use of locally manufactured components above a certain level can endanger both. This would incur a disadvantage to end-users.

Government is concerned with broader policy issues. It is aware that dependence on foreign components inhibits indigenous control over the future of the Brazilian computer industry. Also, it is concerned with the issue of the balance of payments. It therefore has implemented a policy of creating artificial stimulus, such as import quotas and taxes, to induce local firms to source locally.

Government policy is appropriate for the long-term development of the Brazilian computer industry. But the short-term problems associated with its implementation requires local industry protection. Local firms cannot increase the content of locally manufactured components in the face of direct competition with foreign companies, either through imports or local manufacturing by multinationals' subsidiaries and succeed. The contradiction between these concerns is a real problem for policy.

Firms must become aware of the importance of relying more on local components supply. But government must avoid damaging their competitive position. Excluding foreign competition may be the only means to resolving the conflict.

9 ENTRY STRATEGIES OF MULTINATIONAL COMPUTER CORPORATIONS IN BRAZIL

1 INTRODUCTION

This chapter is concerned with the analysis of multinational corporations' entry strategies in the Brazilian computer industry. It examines some of the theoretical hypotheses on multinationals' behaviour which were proposed in Part I.

Chapter 6 described the establishment of non-tariff barriers by Capre in 1976 as part of an effort to set up an indigenous computer manufacturing capability. Entry strategies involve the set of logistic decisions designed by foreign firms to overcome those barriers.

Multinational corporations presence in the Brazilian computer industry takes three different forms: wholly owned subsidiaries, joint ventures and licence agreements. The findings of this study suggest that the forms of entry adopted by multinationals are related to size of the firm and to their policy towards control over foreign operations. Table 9.1 shows the nature of entry and the 1980 value of world-wide DP sales of the multinational firms operating in the Brazilian computer industry.

With respect to size, firms were divided into medium, large and very large. The classification was based on data-processing equipment sales world-wide: less than $200 million (medium); $200–1000 million (large); over $1000 million (very large). Since this classification refers only to firms' data-processing equipment manufacturing activities, multidivisional firms like Ferranti, TWR and NEC are in a smaller category than they would be if their whole range of operations were included.

Control policies for foreign operations were classified into two categories: centralized and decentralized. Firms' policies were defined as centralized when they exercised strict control over both basic[1] and strategic decisions. This meant central control over world-wide marketing (marketing strategies, prices, distribution systems), product policy (product lines, design), production and technical

---
[1] 'Basic' decisions were defined in Chapter 5 as decisions about capital raising and expenditure, dividend policy and organizational policy.

Table 9.1 Foreign computer firms in Brazil 1980

Firm	Country of origin	Nature of entry	World-wide sales in DP market US $1 million	Size classification
IBM	USA	WO subsidiary	21 367	
National Cash Register	USA	WO subsidiary	2840	
Control Data Corporation	USA	Licensing	2790	
Digital Equipment Corporation	USA	WO subsidiary	2743	
Sperry Corporation	USA	WO subsidiary	2552	Very large
Burroughs	USA	WO subsidiary	2478	
Honeywell Inf. Systems	USA	WO subsidiary	1634	
Hewlett-Packard	USA	WO subsidiary	1577	
Fujitsu	Japan	WO & licensing	2756[a]	
Olivetti	Italy	WO subsidiary	2346[a]	
Nippon Electric (NEC)	Japan	Licensing	1000[b]	
Nixdorf	Germany	Licensing	819	
Data General	USA	WO subsidiary	673	
TRW	USA	WO subsidiary	377	
Data Products	USA	Licensing	248	Large
Perkin Elmer	USA	Licensing	226	
Racal Milgo	USA[c]	Joint venture	212	
Shugart	USA	Licensing	200[d]	
Ferranti	UK	JV & licensing	193[e]	
Pertec[f]	USA	Licensing	171[d]	
Ampex	USA	Licensing	170	
Logabax	France	Licensing	160[d]	Medium
Sycor[g]	USA	Licensing	less	
Calcomp	USA	Licensing	than	
Codex	USA	Licensing	200	

Sources: Datamation, firms' annual reports, interviews.

[a]Company's total sales. Includes sectors other than data processing.
[b]Estimate.
[c]American subsidiary of Racal Electronics (UK).
[d]1979.
[e]31 May 1980.
[f]Triumph-Adler (Volkswagen) Group.
[g]Subsidiary of Bell Canada (Canada).

functions (plant design, capital goods, process technology) and procurement policy (components, methods of procurement).

Foreign subsidiaries of most of the centralized multinationals were treated as one 'cog' in the world-wide machine. Manufacturing processes were designed to be compatible throughout the firm world-wide. No one plant manufactured the firm's entire product range, nor even an entire computer system. By global specialization and division of production, the firm obtained world-wide economies of scale.

The findings of this study revealed that most world-leader computer firms tended to adopt such centralized strategies. Firms within this group, however, varied with respect to the scope of their international operations. Some of them centralized their manufacturing facilities in their home country while operating wholly owned marketing subsidiaries in the international market (see Table 9.2).

Table 9.2 Centralized multinationals' entry strategies in the Brazilian computer industry

Firm	Size	Type of operation in data-processing market in Brazil	Entry strategy
IBM	Very large	Manufacturing	Lobby (internal)
Burroughs	Very large	Manufacturing	Lobby (internal)
Hewlett-Packard	Very large	Manufacturing	Lobby (internal)
Data General	Large	Marketing	Lobby (external)
Digital (Dec)	Very large	Marketing	None

The strict policies adopted by centralized firms in relation to their technological and financial assets reflects a desire to obtain monopolistic advantages by the market leaders. Monopoly over technology is particularly important in the market for medium and large computers. A small number of firms dominate the world market.[2] To date, no licensing agreements have been undertaken in this market sector without equity participation being demanded.

Firms have found that some computer technologies are not regular commodities that can be bought in the open market. They are, indeed, different sorts of commodities. A foreign company can choose to produce but not to sell, or it may sell but still retain control.

'Decentralized multinationals' were defined in this study as those companies which had adopted loose control over one or more important basic or logistic decisions. The study found that such firms adopted strict control over some strategies but lose control over the others. 'Decentralized multinationals' may decide, for example, to have local partnership in their foreign subsidiary or even to sell technology to a company in which they have no equity share. Also, they may be flexible with respect to product policy and,

---

[2] In 1973 six firms accounted for 92.8 per cent of the value of the installed base of general-purpose electronic data-processing equipment in the USA. They were: IBM (63.8%), Honeywell (9.4%), Univac (8.1%), Burroughs (5.2%), Control Data (3.6%) and NCR (2.7%). Jequier (1974).

depending on local technological capabilities, manufacture locally designed products. Manufacturing policy may include sub-assembly contracts with other companies and the utilization of different production techniques. Overseas marketing operations may include wholly owned firms, joint ventures and independent distributors.

Hypothesis 3.2 proposed that licenser firms had shifted their preference from equity investment and management control to the sale of technology and management services. Some evidence was found in this study that the scope of flexibility with respect to these issues was related to firms' relative competitive advantages and difficulties. Firms pursued loose control policies when they faced increasing competition, market maintenance and market entry problems. In such situations they took every opportunity to gain access to new markets, to reduce risks, to realize economies of scale and sometimes to gain access to new technologies.

2   ENTRY STRATEGIES

Computer imports into Brazil have become highly selective since 1977. Government approval is required for the import of each computer or peripheral equipment.

The reaction of some multinationals to such a policy was to attempt to set up assembly plants in Brazil. Local manufacture was seen by the firms as a way of avoiding import controls and of gaining access to a protected fast-growing market. In 1977 nine projects were submitted to Capre by foreign firms to obtain permission to import capital goods and components to assemble minicomputers in Brazil. The applicants included those already in the minicomputer market and new entrants such as IBM, Four Phase, Basic Four and TRW. This segment of the market, including minicomputer peripheral equipment, was essentially closed to non-Brazilian manufacturers except through licensing agreements. Consequently, the applications were turned down. Since then, foreign firms have adopted strategies designed to penetrate the market space reserved for Brazilian firms. Four policies were identified in this study. They were lobbying, sales agreements, joint ventures and licensing.

The analysis proceeded into two steps. The former two strategies, which are pursued by a relatively small number of firms, were examined and analysed based on information collected during interviews and from the specialized press. However, the latter two entry strategies—joint venture and licensing—were explored statistically. This was necessary because of the large number of variables to be analysed compared with the first group. Twenty-one firms were selected for inclusion in the analysis. They did not simply constitute a random sample of multinational computer firms in Brazil, they in fact constitute almost all the installed base of computers in Brazil. Together they accounted for 94 per cent of the 1979 installed base, either directly or through licensing agreements.

(a) The lobby policy

The main features of this policy is lobbying to obtain permission to import kits and components to assemble computers in Brazil. Since minicomputer manufacturing is closed to non-Brazilian firms, foreign firms introduced products which were 'border-line' mini and medium-range computers. Computer-range definitions are somewhat arbitrary, since prices and costs are falling and capacity increasing continuously. Some multinationals have taken advantage of this in order to penetrate the Brazilian minicomputer market.

Since 1978 some multinationals have assumed the role of 'victims' of the 'market reserve policy'. They have alleged that they were discriminated against by the government's decision to exclude them from the minicomputer industry. This tactic achieved some success. In November 1978 Capre authorized IBM to manufacture a new computer model—the newly developed 4341. IBM introduced this model as a substitute for the mid-range 148 computer and accepted Capre's demand that three computers should be exported for each one placed in the internal market.

In August 1980 IBM succeeded in obtaining approval from SEI to assemble the 4331 MG2 model. This was cheaper and had a smaller memory capacity than the 4341. The approval might have been the result of intense lobby pressure as the 4331 (called 'Ipanema' by IBM) had been turned down twice before—once in 1978 in the case of the 4341 model and again in May 1980.

Export requirements for the 4331 were substantially reduced. IBM had to export one and a half computers for each placed in the local market. Despite its medium-range classification, the 4331 can indirectly compete with minicomputers, particularly because of leasing conditions offered to its customers. IBM has been authorized to sell locally up to 242 units of the 4331 to its present customers. This represents almost US $60 million in sales of central processor units alone.

In 1980 Burroughs was given permission to introduce its newly developed B-6900 computer in the Brazilian market. The model was presented to SEI as a substitute for the B-6800 line which was already being assembled in Brazil. The authorization included disk-drive units.

Hewlett-Packard was also authorized to import capital goods and components in order to assemble and market microcomputers in Brazil. The project had been rejected previously but HP had found a loophole in SEI regulations preventing foreign companies from producing microcomputers for commercial use. HP was negotiating a deal which would allow it to sell models designed for technical and scientific applications. Domestic manufacturers complained that the machines could be put to commercial use, but HP gave an assurance that it would withhold the necessary software.

Another important entry strategy was adopted for peripheral equipment. It consisted of obtaining permission to assemble line printers in Brazil exclusively for export. Along with local manufacture, firms began to offer the equipment in the local market without immediately delivering it. After collecting a large number of orders, the firm asked the government for permission to import assembled printers in order to meet customers' demands. Supplying customers through local production was then presented as an import-saving alternative.

This strategy was successfully pursued by IBM. In 1980 it was granted permission to supply Brazilian customers with a fixed amount of printer units which were intended for export. In the light of IBM's success in penetrating a market officially reserved for Brazilian firms, Burroughs was also encouraged to enter the Brazilian computer printer market. In 1981 it was authorized to sell in Brazil low-speed (50 cps) printer mechanisms manufactured for export only.

Another market segment that is threatened by the multinationals is the low-price end of the word-processor market. The Brazilian firm MDA developed a product based on IBM electric typewriters to which an electronic kit and a floppy-disk drive were added. Olivetti, which also manufactures electrical typewriters in Brazil, has already announced its intention to sell a similar product. The model will probably not depend on direct imports and consequently not depend on import quotas. If Olivetti succeeds in selling word processors openly in Brazil, IBM could follow the same path and MDA would probably be driven out of the market.

Identification of the elements which encouraged multinationals to challenge government policies is of major importance. Even more important are the implications of the challenge. A major reason for such a challenge is the firms' strength. The risky strategy of selling products that could not be legally delivered under current government regulations is one which only financially and commercially strong corporations can afford to pursue. This policy, in fact, was pursued unsuccessfully by IBM in the past. In 1977 the corporation assembled and sold more than 400 System 32 minicomputers in Brazil before having its manufacturing project rejected by Capre. In the following year IBM requested permission to supply its customers with imported models but this was also rejected by the government. According to Brazilian minicomputer manufacturers, Burroughs also offered equipment which was not approved by the government (*Jornal do Brasil*, 17 April 1979, p. 24).

This has a negative psychological effect on local industry. It can prevent the sales of products by Brazilian firms while customers wait for the government's final decision. Customers may also form a lobby in support of multinationals if they really need their products. On the other hand, this policy involves marketing costs which may not be recuperable. But this cost may not be so prohibitive for some very large multinationals who already have regular contact with their customers.

A second reason for challenging government policies is export capacity. Two firms demonstrated great flexibility in their range of decisions concerning international trade. In the case of minicomputer System 32, IBM had already assembled a large number of models in Brazil. After Capre's decision to turn down the project, they appeared to have little difficulty in exporting elsewhere. Medium-sized or decentralized firms might not be able to do this.

Export requirements themselves also encouraged lobbying for the balance of payments deficit is one of the most urgent economic problems in Brazil. Only large multinationals with centralized, world-wide, decision-making processes can adequately meet the Brazilian government's requirement for a large volume of exports.

The relative importance of these centralized multinationals in Brazilian manufacturing industry is another factor supporting their entry strategies in the computer industry. IBM and Burroughs have a total employment of 8000 people in Brazil and sales in 1979 were almost half a billion dollars (see Table 9.3). Both companies have long-establshed teams of Brazilian senior managers who can undertake successful lobbying. Contracts with government are generally at the highest level. In 1977, when Capre was about to take a decision on minicomputer manufacturing policy, a senior international management team from IBM was received by former-president Ernesto Geisel himself.

Table 9.3 IBM and Burroughs in Brazil

Firm	Sales ($1000)	Exports ($1000)	Employees
IBM	400 000[a]	92 400	5020
Burroughs	92 826	15 900	3044
Total	492 826	108 300	8064

Sources: *Gazeta Mercantil*, September 1979.
  QUEM e QUEM na Economia Brasileira, 1980.
  [a]1978.

Home country lobbying policies

One centralized multinational—Data General (DG)—even adopted a strategy of lobbying its home country's government to put pressure on the Brazilian government concerning non-tariff import barriers.

Although it is the second largest minicomputer manufacturer in the world,[3] DG has achieved little penetration in Brazil. It has expanded its international business through export of its US-designed and manufactured products. According to DG there are no basic cost advantages in foreign manufacture, either directly or through licensing, of minicomputers. It believes that it would not be advantageous to manufacture abroad in the future. DG gave two reasons for this: first, the greater inflation rates in developing countries; second, the electronic miniaturization tendency of their basic products. Soon a few microprocessors will incorporate most functions required by mainframe computers due to very-large-scale integrated semiconductors (VLSI).

In June 1977 DG presented a paper to the US President's Special Representative for Trade Negotiations (SRT) complaining of the 'discriminatory international trade practices' adopted by Brazil. DG stated that such a policy would adversely affect American minicomputer companies. Further, they claimed the success of the Brazilian policy would encourage other nations to follow suit. According to DG, the governments of Japan, Yugoslavia, certain European Nations, the Soviet Union and Eastern bloc nations were already following similar policies.

DG suggested that the American government should adopt the following steps in relation to Brazil:

[3] In 1980 DG international sales of minicomputers totalled US $673 million. It was the second largest independent minicomputer manufacturer after Digital Equipment Corporation (DEC).

1) Bilaterally request that Brazil eliminate tariff and non-tariff barriers on U.S. minicomputers in exchange for shelving retaliatory U.S. barriers on Brazilian imports into the U.S.
2) Bilaterally request that Brazil eliminate technology transfer requirements for granting manufacturing licences to U.S. firms in exchange for granting U.S. approval for such manufacturing licences.
3) Establishment of U.S. regulations prohibiting ownership transfer of computer technology (hardware and software) to any wholly-owned foreign firm, but permitting manufacturing licences.
4) Establishment of U.S. regulations prohibiting foreign government agreements with U.S. firms providing them exclusive exemption from import quotas or licences.

(J. B. Stroup, Manager, Financial & Public Affairs, 12 May 1977)

This seems to have had little effect. In 1979 the President's SRT asked the Brazilian Embassy in Washington to inform him about computer import restrictions in Brazil. He stated that the Brazilian policy was particularly affecting one American minicomputer manufacturer. The matter was further discussed at the November 1979 meeting of the Consultative Subgroup for Brazil-US Trade. According to *Relatorio Reservado* (Number 683, p. 1) the Brazilian Foreign Ministry informed SRT that import control was only a provisional measure in view of Brazilian balance of payment difficulties.

Implications of the lobby policies

The major implications of the 'lobby policies' adopted by some centralized multinationals to counter the 'reserved market' will now be discussed.

A benefit of local manufacture by centralized multinationals, is that customers can enjoy a wider range of product choice. Customers may benefit from the entry-phase incentives offered by multinationals. These include better price and payment conditions and a high standard of product quality and performance.

Large multinationals also may temporarily provide better export performance than locally owned computer firms. The evidence suggests, however, that the contribution of local subsidiaries of computer multinationals to the improvement of the Brazilian balance of payments may not be significant in the long term, because products manufactured locally by MNCs' subsidiaries present substantially lower content of local components than locally designed products. IBM and Burroughs recently began to export more than they import (see Table 9.4). But this is not the case if imports of assembled equipment directly imported by customers are included.

Table 9.4 IBM and Burroughs balance of trade in Brazil, 1973-9 (US $1000)

Year	IBM			Burroughs		
	Exports	Imports	Balance	Exports	Imports	Balance
1973	n.a.	n.a.	n.a.	8588	n.a.	n.a.
1974	54 297	83 670	(29 473)	11 072	33 100	(22 028)
1975	n.a.	n.a.	n.a.	11 832	n.a.	n.a.
1976	n.a.	n.a.	n.a.	2727	n.a.	n.a.
1977	44 608	35 524	9084	10 573	n.a.	n.a.
1978	82 525	52 325	30 200	15 898	12 595	3303
1979	92 360	56 536	35 823	n.a.	n.a.	n.a.

The disadvantages of the expansion of foreign firms in the Brazilian medium-range computer market, are the limits to the development of indigenous technology. Cobra has recently launched its new medium-sized computer, Cobra 530, which has been totally designed and developed in Brazil. But the sales potential of the series, which covers a range of core sizes between 512 KB and 1 MB, will be seriously affected by the decision to allow IBM to manufacture the larger 4331 model in Brazil. The problem for Cobra is that the new IBM computer, though larger than its own 530 model, has been competitively priced.

All the other major Brazilian computer manufacturers are planning to introduce medium-sized computers with core sizes between 512 KB and 1 MB. These include Sisco (MC 9700), SID (SID 5800), Labo (8038 and 8043) and Edisa which signed an agreement with NCE/UFRJ (Rio de Janeiro Federal University) to manufacture the PDP 11/70 DEC—a compatible computer developed by the latter.

Despite their larger size (the IBM 4331 model has a minimum core size of 2 MB), IBM computers may capture a large share of the Brazilian computer manufacturers' market. IBM has a strong marketing base and the financial capacity to rent or lease the new computers at a lower price/rent ratio than its Brazilian competitors. The manufacturers of peripheral products, such as 80 MB tapes and print-out machines, will also be affected. They have been relying on high Cobra sales but now fear that their market will be narrowed. Their links with Cobra and other local manufacturers have brought them into direct competition with IBM.

SEI limited the sale of the model 4331 to replacements for existing installed IBM machines (models 360 and 370) that have become obsolete. This is estimated at 250 customers. However, according to

Abicomp (Brazilian Computer Industry Association), along with replacing the 4331, IBM will take back equipment which is currently rented to its customers. This will then be offered in the second-hand market at very competitive prices (*JB*, 10 August 1980).

There have been increasing complaints about the manufacturing authorization for the HP 85 desk-top microcomputer. Hewlett-Packard views the HP 85 as specifically oriented to scientific applications and not as a competitor to locally manufactured microcomputers oriented to commercial applications. Local manufacturers, however, believe that commercial applications for the HP 85 could be developed either by HP itself or by customers, in particular by the 'System Houses'. The HP 85 would then compete directly with several locally developed microcomputers. These include Cobra 300, Polymax 101-SS, SID 3000, Micro-Scopus and Prologica 700. According to Abicomp, the HP 85 is cheaper than locally developed products because it utilizes LSI custom microchips specially designed for it. Local industry does not have the volume of orders and the resources to justify the development of special microchips and thus is found to rely on general-purpose semiconductors.

IBM and Burroughs plans to manufacture locally and sell printer units locally may also have negative effects on the Brazilian computer peripherals industry. The USA companies will compete directly with three Brazilian printer manufacturers: Elebra Informatica, Globus and Digilab.

The business practices adopted by foreign multinationals to keep their market shares in the markets officially reserved for Brazilian firms lend support to the hypothesis (Hyp. 1.2) that direct investment by MNCs in developing countries restrains competition and imposes barriers to entry for indigenous firms.

(b) Sales agreement policy

Entry strategies based on sales agreements are adopted by multinationals whose comparative strength in the Brazilian minicomputer market is primarily due to their marketing capabilities. The strategy involves agreements with a Brazilian firm to manufacture a product on an exclusive basis and sell it under its own brand name. The main characteristic of this strategy is the holding of loose control over product policy.

The sales agreement policy had been pursued by Olivetti even before the import control measures. Olivetti market a data-entry system (DE 520) in Brazil which was manufactured by Sycor in the

USA. The product was jointly developed by the firms but sold world-wide by Olivetti on an exclusive basis.

The first sales agreement designed to secure entry in the face of market restriction was reached in 1979 between Olivetti[4] and the Brazilian firm Scopus. Previously Olivetti had several requests to establish manufacturing prospects rejected. Scopus and Olivetti jointly developed a data-entry system for which Olivetti provides the software and Scopus the hardware. The product, DE 1500 BR, also incorporated a printer and magnetic-tape drive manufactured by Globus and floppy-disk drive supplied by Flexidisk on an OEM (Original Equipment Manufacturer) basis. Olivetti also negotiated a similar agreement with the Brazilian firm Prologica to market an electronic accounting machine developed and produced by the latter. Prologica also provides the foreign firm RUF with the electronic accounting machine 'Data Ruf 324 (see Table 9.5).

Table 9.5 DP industry's sales agreements between local firms and multinational corporations' subsidiaries

MNC subsidiary	Local firm	Product under sales agreement	% of local firms' output under sales agreements
Olivetti	Scopus	Data entry (DE 1500 BR)	10%
	Prologica	Electronic accounting machine	25%
ICL (Friden)	Hybrid	Electronic accounting machine	
RUF	Prologica	Electronic accounting machine	25%
Ecodata (Cable Wireless)	Parks	Video display unit	25%

Two other multinationals adopted sales agreement strategy as a means to market entry in Brazil. International Computers Limited (ICL) has a marketing agreement with the Brazilian manufacturer Hybrid to sell an electronic accounting machine under the brand name Friden. Ecodata, a subsidiary of Cable Wireless (UK) signed an agreement in November 1980 with the Brazilian firm Parks to manufacture 250 VDUs developed by the British company. The

[4] Olivetti is considering simultaneously adopting other strategies (such as joint venture) to secure its position in the Brazilian minicomputer market.

terminals will be connected to the CCI—Consolidated Computer Incorporation—minicomputer imported into Brazil by Ecodata.

Implications of sales agreement entry strategy

Sales agreement strategy has been creating some concern in the industry. Such agreements have the advantage of providing local partners with a well-established marketing network. Firms like Olivetti can afford to develop the market through the provision of leasing and customer financing. However, sales agreements also have negative effects. Abicomp considered that such agreements may disrupt the market reserve policy. If other segments of the market were included under sales agreements multinationals could regain market leadership. Effective market control could be a means to technological and manufacturing control. Abicomp was especially concerned with the re-entry of Olivetti to segments of the data-processing market which were being developed by several Brazilian firms. Olivetti already had a large customer base and widespread marketing facilities in Brazil.

Brazilian firms could become dependent on their sales partners. However, this can be prevented by policies setting limits to such agreements' shares of local firms' total sales. Scopus limited their deliveries to Olivetti to up to 10 per cent of total output. Prologica reduced its sales to Olivetti and RUF from 80 to 50 per cent of total output. It is developing a policy of direct sales in order to reduce further its dependence to 25 per cent.

(c) Joint-venture policies

By 1981 three foreign computer companies were associated in joint ventures with local groups. Racal Milgo Inc (American subsidiary of Racal Electronics UK) has a 49 per cent partnership in the modem manufacturer Coencisa Industria de Comunicacoes SA. In 1980 Ferranti Ltd (UK) set up a system and software company in a 49–51 per cent partnership with Mayrink Veiga & Cia Ltd. Ferranti also holds a small interest in Cobra (about 3 per cent of total shares). In May 1981 CII-Honeywell Bull (France) set up a mainframe computer manufacturing firm in association with two local groups. The firm called Telematica is 40 per cent owned by CII-Honeywell Bull and assembles computers ranging from 2 to 8 MB of memory capacity. The two Brazilian groups (Pereira Lopes and Brazilinvest) had no previous experience in computers and all product and process technology is provided by CII-HB.

Joint venture may become an important entry strategy for other foreign firms restricted by local policies. Olivetti, Sperry Univac, Burroughs, Control Data, and other multinationals were announcing plans to introduce local capital into their local subsidiaries. These firms believe that a majority of local ownership would improve their relationship with the government and possibly allow them to overcome barriers to direct market entry. Table 9.6 outlines foreign firms' ownership *preferences* in the Brazilian computer sector. These were determined on the basis of interviews, projects submitted to the government, attitudes and strategies adopted in other countries.

Table **9.6** Multinationals' ownership preferences in the Brazilian computer sector

Ownership structure	First Preference	Second Preference	Form of ownership actually undertaken
Wholly owned subsidiary	16	–	9
Joint ventures	2	11	1
Licensing	3	3	11
None/Unknown	–	7	–
Total	21	21	21

Of 21 multinational firms, only two would adopt joint venture as their first ownership preference if given a choice. The following reasons were pointed out for preferring wholly owned subsidiaries: financial weakness of local partners, short-term view of returns, difficulty in managing the operations and loose control over decisions.

These results lend support to the hypothesis (Hyp. 3.1) which states that MNCs preference is to offer a 'package' of equity investment, managerial skills and technical knowledge rather than just license their know-how.

In Table 9.1 only five of 21 firms were considered 'centralized multinationals'. The remaining 16 met the definition of 'decentralized multinationals'. Ten firms were very large and 11 large or medium. Another distinction was made between firms which submitted projects to the government to set up manufacturing plants in Brazil (8 firms) and those which had not pursued this entry strategy (13 firms). Table 9.7 shows that of the 21 firms in the survey, 11 had at least one joint-venture subsidiary in another country. The relationship between ownership strategy (actually undertaken, preferred and adopted in other countries), control over foreign operations,

Table 9.7 Overseas joint-venture subsidiaries of MNCs which operate in Brazil

Company	Name of firm	Country	Partner	Partnership (%)
Ampex Corp.	Aurex SA	Mexico		50
	APG Electronica[a]	Brazil		49
Control Data Corp.	Magnetic Peripheral	USA	Honeywell Inf. Syst.	70
	Comp. Peripheral Inc.	USA	NCR, ICL	33
	Control Dataset	UK	ICL	75
	Computer Terminal	Iran		30
	ROM Control Data	Rumania	Rumanian government	45
Ferranti Ltd	Cobra SA	Brazil	Brazilian government	3.0
	Sistemas Ferranti		Mayrink Veiga	49
	do Brasil Ltda	Brazil		
	Ferranti Eastman	Switzerland		51
Fujitsu Ltd	Amdahl	USA	Amdahl, Nixdorf	28
	TRW-Fujitsu	USA	TRW Datacom	51
	—	WG	Siemens	
	—	Spain	Spanish Postal Service	
Hewlett-Packard	—	Spain		50
Honeywell Inf. System	Magnetic Peripheral	USA	Control Data	30
	CII-Honeywell Bull	France	Cie Machine Bull	47
	Telematica[b]	Brazil	Pereira Lopes Brazilinvest	40

Company	Subsidiary/Venture	Country	Partner	%
ICL—International Computer Ltd	Control Dataset	UK	Control Data	25
	Computer Peripheral	USA	NCR, Control Data	33
Nippon Electric (NEC)[a]	Gold Star Electric	Korea		
	Irano-Nippon Electronics Ind.	Iran	Iranian private	
	Pernas NEC Multip.	Malaysia		
	Rank-Nec Pty Ltd	Australia		
	Cia Electr. Nacional	Brazil	Docas de Santos	49
	Taiwan Telecom.	Taiwan		
Nixdorf	Amdahl	USA	Amdahl, Fujitsu	
Racal Milgo Inc	ICC-Coencisa	Brazil	Coencisa	49
TRW Datacom	TRW-Fujitsu Co.	USA	Fujitsu	49
	Datacom Iberia	Spain	Sener Ingeneria Sistema SA	
	Ventek Ltd	UK	Canada Dev. Corp.	
	Matra Informatique	France	Matra SA	
	Sigma Data Corp.	Australia		
Olivetti SpA	Memorax Corp.	USA		
	Mafra	France		

[a]Not in data-processing equipment business.
[b]Under negotiation.

and size was also explored statistically. Figure 9.1 gives bivariate correlations (Yules' Q) between variables collapsed into dichotomous categories. The correlation coefficients were subjected to the chi-square test under the same set of assumptions made in Chapter 7.[5]

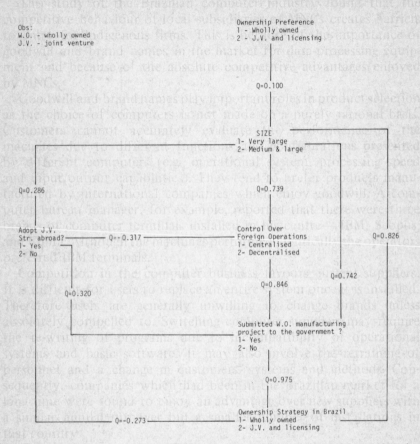

Fig. 9.1 Multinational corporations' ownership strategy, size and control in the Brazilian computer sector

Centralized firms tend to be very large (Q = 0.739) and tend to prefer wholly owned subsidiaries. Correlation between control over foreign operations and the submission of projects to establish wholly owned manufacturing subsidiaries in Brazil is fairly high (Q = 0.846).

Only very large multinationals set up wholly owned subsidiaries (Q = 0.826). Smaller firms either licensed their technology or

[5] Two nominal scales and one degree of freedom.

entered into joint ventures in order to compete in the Brazilian market. However, the relationship between size and ownership preference is not significant (Q = 0.100). We may conclude that the majority of firms *preferred* wholly owned subsidiaries irrespective of size. But only very large firms *could* actually afford to pursue this strategy. This is supported by the high correlation between size and the submission of wholly owned manufacturing projects to the government (Q = 0.742).

Computer multinationals adopted different ownership strategies in Brazil compared with other countries, since the correlation between these is not significant (Q = −0.273). This means that some MNCs adopted joint ventures in other countries but did not pursue this strategy in Brazil. This was either because they found it relatively less advantageous or because they were not required to do so by the Brazilian government.

In the case of entry in the highly competitive Japanese market, one US firm located in Brazil considered that a Japanese partner with a well-established marketing network would be required. But they might not adopt the same strategy in Brazil, where competitive conditions in the computer industry were not so difficult.

Burroughs, however, has been buying out its computer manufacturing partners in Japan, since that country's government began to liberalize entry conditions. Burroughs recently announced that it would be prepared to accept local partnership in its Brazilian subsidiary if this reduced government interference in its local activities. In Burrough's case joint ventures were directly related to local government policies.

Large multinational computer firms insist on absolute control over the management of transfers between partly or wholly owned overseas affiliates and the rest of the company world-wide. Transfers are in the form of inputs to the affiliate: technology and other resources as well as the supply of components or semifinished products. They are also in the form of outputs from the affiliate: products, as well as dividends and other financial flows.

(d) Licensing policy

Licensing agreements involving technical and industrial co-operation between Brazilian and foreign firms have played a major role in the development of the local computer industry. In 1974 the first licensing agreement for computer technology was signed between the British company Ferranti Ltd and Cobra. Since 1977, when government policy became more clearly defined, newly established

Brazilian firms have been shopping around for computer technology. By 1980 18 agreements had been signed, involving 16 foreign and 14 local firms (see Table 9.8).

Table 9.8 Licensing agreements between Brazilian and foreign firms for computer and peripheral technology

Licenser	Size	Year	Product	Licensee
Ferranti Ltd	M	1974	Minicomputer	Cobra
Sycor Inc	M	1976	Minicomputer	Cobra
Nixdorf	L	1977	Minicomputer	Labo Eletronica
Logabax	M	1978	Minicomputer	SID
Fujitsu	VL	1978	Minicomputer	Edisa
Racal Milgo[a]	M	1976	Modem	ICC-Coencisa
NEC	L	1977	Modem	OZ Eletronica
Codex	M	1978	Modem	Elebra Eletronica
Honeywell	VL	1977	Printer	Elebra Informatica
NEC	L	1978	Printer	Digilab
Data Products	M	1979	Printer	Globus
Ampex Corporation	M	1978	Disk and tape drive	Microlab
Control Data	VL	1978	Disk drive	Elebra Informatica
PCC-Pertec	M	1979	Disk drive	Multidigit
Calcomp	M	1978	Floppy-disk drive	Cobra
Shugart Associates	L	1979	Floppy-disk drive	Flexidisk
PCC-Pertec	M	1978	Tape drive	Globus
Parkin Elmer	M	1980	Tape drive	Compart

[a]Licensing agreement and joint venture.
M – Medium; L – Large; VL – Very Large.

It was found that medium-size foreign firms entered into licensing agreements more readily than larger foreign firms. Medium-size firms usually lacked the managerial and financial resources to compete directly in overseas markets. A licensing agreement did not require any additional investment and helped the firms to recover previous R & D expenditure. Licensing has opened an export market for kits and components and represents a source of royalty payments. Business generated through such agreements has come to play an important role in foreign firms' export markets. One example is the California-based Pertec Computer Corporation. After its two agreements with Brazilian firms, Pertec's business in Brazil became larger than in the whole Pacific area.

Of the 16 multinational corporations which licensed Brazilian companies, only three were very large (see Table 9.7). Two of them —Control Data and Fujitsu—had only small shares of the Brazilian market and the third—Honeywell—licensed only peripheral equipment technology. Other large minicomputer manufactures, like DEC and Data General, were involved in licensing negotiations, but they required very strict technology transfer conditions which were not accepted by their Brazilian partners.

Only two licensing agreements involved the sale of equity shares. In another six, licensers had asked for equity participation in licensed firms but it was not accepted by local firms because of government regulations.

At least 10 firms had licensing agreements in other countries (see Table 9.9). Japan led with six contracts, followed by the USA (5 agreements), East European countries (4 agreements), China (3

Table 9.9 Licensing agreements in other countries by firms which licensed Brazilian companies

Licenser	Licensee	Country	Type of agreement
Honeywell	NEC	Japan	Cross-licensing
	Toshiba	Japan	Cross-licensing
Fujitsu	Hitachi	Japan	Cross-licensing
	Amdhal	USA	Cross-licensing
NEC	Toshiba	Japan	Cross-licensing
Shugart	TTA	Japan	Sub-assembly agreement
	CPU Computers	UK	
Data Products	Videoton	Hungary	Licensing only
	Marubeni	Japan	Licensing only
Logabax	Comp. Periph. Inc.,[a] 1973	USA	Licensing only
	Sycor, 1973	USA	Licensing only
	–	China[b]	Licensing only
	Siemens, 1975	W. Germany	Licensing only
	Mera Metronex, 1972, 1974, 1976	Poland	Licensing only
Sycor	Olivetti	Italy	Cross-licensing
Ferranti	–	China	Licensing only
Ampex	–	China[b]	Licensing only
	–	Rumania	Licensing only
PCC-Pertec	–	Rumania	Licensing only
Nixdorf	Memorex	USA	
	Control Data	USA	
	Elbit Computer	Israel	

[a]Joint venture between NCR, Control Data and ICL.
[b]Under negotiation.

agreements), and three EEC countries and Israel with one agreement each. Some of the contracts with American and Japanese firms involved a reverse flow of technology in the form of cross-licensing agreements.

None of the firms which licensed Brazilian computer firms had technology transfer agreements in other developing countries. They supplied these markets through distributors or through wholly owned subsidiaries.

There are two kinds of strategy adopted by multinational firms in exploiting their technology abroad. One strategy is adopted by the 'centralized multinationals' and the other by the decentralized firms. The hypothesis of Hymer and Caves (Hyp. 3.1) that licenser firms' preference is to offer a 'package' of capital, managerial skills and technical knowledge, rather than just licence their know-how, is essentially valid for most multinational computer firms. But only large centralized firms can successfully insist upon this.

The alternative hypothesis developed by Baranson (Hyp. 3.2) that multinationals have shifted their preference from equity investment and management control to sale of technology and management services applies only to medium and small computer firms. These are more adaptable to the demands of newly industrialized countries for technology sharing. They also lack the capabilities necessary to overcome entry barriers and to compete directly with world-wide industry leaders abroad.

10   CONTROL AND PACKAGING STRATEGIES OF LICENSING AGREEMENTS IN THE BRAZILIAN COMPUTER INDUSTRY

In Chapters 4 and 5 it was suggested that licensing agreements might constrain the independence of local firms. This chapter examines the extent and implications of such agreements in the Brazilian computer industry. The analysis is based on an evaluation of the influence which technology suppliers can exercise over licensees' strategic decisions.[1] Influence can be exercised through the nature and extent of managerial and technical assistance provided.

1   MANAGERIAL ASSISTANCE

Managerial assistance relates to organizational policy, capital raising, expenditure advice and marketing policy. The findings of this study suggest that managerial assistance is not an important factor in licensing agreements between Brazilian and foreign computer firms. Of the 11 multinational firms studied, only one appeared to involve major influence over its licensee's basic managerial decisions (see Table 10.1). Most of the local firms were already well-established industrial companies or were themselves able to obtain the necessary managerial skills to establish their own organizational policy.

The influence of licensers was clearly visible in relation to capital raising and expenditure advice. But generally this does not give them any significant control over licensees. Some multinationals gave expenditure advice, for example, with respect to the value of investment required, size of manufacturing area to be purchased, etc., while others provided short-term credit for the supply of component parts to licensees. However, this was a normal commercial practice rather than a mechanism of control over licensees' capital-raising policy.

[1] The analysis includes 11 multinational firms which account for almost 70 per cent of all technology transfer agreements signed in the computer sector. It included interviews and review of agreements of technical information, assistance and training between Brazilian and foreign firms.

Table 10.1 Licensers' influence over licensees' managerial decisions in the Brazilian Computer Industry

Managerial assistance provided	Number of firms		
	Yes	No	Total
Organizational policy	1	10	11
Capital raising and expenditure advice	1	10	11
Marketing policy	6	5	11

Marketing policy was the most popular form of managerial assistance to licensees. Six multinationals provided this for their licensees. This included transfer of staff from the licenser to help establish marketing facilities, provision of training for the licensee's marketing personnel and assistance in marketing evaluation.

Marketing assistance does not necessarily imply control over licensees' decisions in this respect. However, it may give licensers the decision-making power to impose constraints upon licensees' marketing policies. In the Brazilian computer industry constraints upon licensees' freedom were imposed through export prohibitions to specific countries or a ban on all exports. These conditions were not included in the formal agreement themselves, because of regulations concerning technology transfer agreements, but were found in unwritten agreements between the partners. One licenser claimed that:

We control the production and shipping of important component parts, and (we) know how many products can be sold in Brazil. If our licensee exports from Brazil, we might consider cutting component part supply to them.

Two licensees were able to export final products but they were not authorized to sell on an Original Equipment Manufacturer (OEM) basis. They could export some equipment embodied in a computer system but this kind of export was unlikely to become very significant. This is a severe competitive constraint as most international sales of peripheral equipment are done on an OEM basis.

2   TECHNICAL ASSISTANCE

The transfer of documentation to licensees is an important means of technical assistance. Documentation involves the supply of product manuals, product specifications, designs, layout and manufacturing process instructions. Technical assistance may also involve provision of training for licensees' personnel.

At least two technology suppliers preferred agreements which included the whole set of information concerning product design, plant design, specifications of equipment and tools, component parts and marketing strategies. One firm saw this as the need to 'take care of' their licensees. The other explained that in package deals licensees have no need to be concerned with product design, specifications and process technology. They are able to concentrate on supervision only.

One consequence of this form of control was constraints upon the use of alternative technology. One agreement included the following clause:

During the duration of the agreement, the licensee shall not manufacture or sell any equipment which would be competitive with the licensed products without licensers approval.

This requirement could significantly reduce the possibility of the firm becoming technologically independent.

The extent of 'packaging' in technology transfer agreements depends on the capabilities of the recipient companies. Some companies begin with package deals but move on to introduce technical inputs of their own as they acquire expertise.

Table 10.2 shows the different forms of technical assistance

Table 10.2 Technical assistance provided in licensing agreements in the Brazilian computer industry

Type of assistance	Number of agreements		
	Some	None	Total
Quality control	9	2	11
Improvement in licensed products	7	4	11
Improvement in process techniques	6	5	11
Information about new equipment	4	7	11
Procurement policy	9	2	11
Factory design	5	6	11

provided in licensing agreements in the Brazilian computer industry. These are quality control, improvement in licensed products and in process technologies, information about new equipment, procurement policy and factory design.

Quality control

Most of the agreements included the provision of methods of quality control. In some cases this included the sale of testing equipment developed by the licensers, but this was limited by the scale of the operations. Some automatic testing equipment utilized by large volume producers was not viable for small-scale operations. The different cost of some inputs, e.g. labour, may encourage the adoption of alternative quality control methods.

Control can be exercised through clauses reserving for licensers the right to exercise authority over quality control to ensure quality standards of licensed products. Such clauses were found in two agreements. This would affect local firms' capacity to make substantial product change without licensers' approval.

Improvements in licensed products

Some licensees lack the necessary expertise to adopt an independent product policy and therefore they have to rely on licensers for further developments of licensed products. Through improvements to licensed products, licensers may exercise control over licensees' technical decisions. This may lead to permanent links between the partners and therefore to technological dependence.

However, regular contact between the contracting partners regarding the licensed product may not necessarily produce dependence. Two Brazilian firms were able independently to improve minicomputers produced under licence and develop new applications. They now supply information to their licensers, particularly in relation to software technology.

About two-thirds of the technology suppliers in the Brazilian computer industry informed firms about improvement in licensed products, but licensees were not necessarily required to adopt them. In only one agreement was there a clause obliging the licensees to ask the licenser for approval for any modifications to licensed products.

If a modification in a licensed product involved major product change, a new contract was required. However, minor modifications to licensed products were usually included under the existing agreements.

Improvements in process techniques and information about equipment

More than half the licensers informed licensees about modifications in process techniques. Approximately one-third gave details about some of the new equipment introduced in their own production lines. Most of the information about manufacturing process technology was provided during the start-up phase. Licensers usually provided further information when asked to do so. This included problem-solving assistance and regular meetings to discuss problems involving process techniques.

Procurement policy

The sourcing of components is the most important aspect of computer firms' procurement policies. Reliance on a single supplier may result in overpricing. It may also constrain a firm's ability to absorb and further develop imported technology.

Computer products have a very short life cycle. Some firms launch new peripheral equipment every two or three years. Dependence on the supply of component parts from licensers may force the firm to depend on licensers for product policy as well.

Many technology suppliers claimed that their licensees would rely on some component parts manufactured by them throughout the duration of the agreement (five years). The manufacture of some key components, for example printers' hammers and magnetic heads for disk drive, requires high-technology manufacturing equipment, a highly skilled labour force and high standards of quality control. Small-scale local consumption was not sufficient to encourage the investment required to produce such key components in Brazil. Consequently, local firms relied on technology suppliers to obtain them. Licensers therefore enjoyed a position of quasi-monopoly, because components supplied by another firm were not compatible. If a licenser's product which incorporates key components is phased-out, licensees would have no alternative but to follow the product change. This may require another five-year agreement and the reinforcement and extension of technology dependence.

Most licensees in Brazil buy 100 per cent of their imported components directly from their licensers. This may be due to the fact that, at the time of this study a large number of them were entering the SKD phase of manufacturing. This involves the purchase of kits which are assembled locally. Most agreements establish a minimum fixed number of kits to be purchased from licensers. During the CKD phase, when parts are purchased on a CKD basis, some licensees may retain independence to choose alternative sources of component parts supply.

Nine of the eleven multinationals studied influenced licensees' overseas procurement policy. This did not extend to local supply, where licensers had virtually no influence on licensees' purchasing policies. Thus, the more 'nationalized' the product, the more independent were the local firms with respect to procurement policy.

Manufacturing plant design

Manufacturing plant design and development are usually incorporated to the sale of machinery and process technology. Advisers can both suggest equipment for purchase and sell a project 'package' which incorporates other inputs tied to the licenser.

Plant design does not play an important role in technology transfer agreements in the Brazilian computer industry. Less than half of the agreements included any kind of advice on plant design. There are four reasons for this.

First, the scale of operations of local plants were considerably smaller than those of the technology suppliers. Advanced techniques adopted in licensers' factories, such as, automatic insertion of components on circuit boards and computerized assembly control, cannot be justified in small-scale operations. Second, different relative costs of labour, equipment, materials and other inputs made feasible the adoption of different process techniques to those adopted by licensers. Third, many Brazilian licensees were well-established manufacturing firms. They were able to undertake the manufacture of licensed products with existing facilities, and where this was not possible they often had the expertise to develop an entirely new plant independently of advice from licensers. Fourth, the Brazilian computer industry at an early stage of development, emphasized product rather than process technology. Plant design therefore played a secondary role in local firms' technology supply priorities. But this may change with the increasing quality and cost/price competition between firms and the establishment of a larger production base. This will increase pressures for process innovation and for manufacturing efficiency (Sciberras, 1980).

3   THE RENEWAL OF LICENSING AGREEMENTS

Most technology suppliers to the Brazilian computer industry argued that there was a bilateral interest in introducing new products and renewing licensing agreements. But this could lead to an increase in technological dependence. The need for new agreements could be a reflection of the inability or unwillingness of the local firm to design and develop its own product line, or of the capacity of the licenser to control the licensees' product policy.

Eight out of eleven licensers saw technology links with Brazilian companies as long-term relationships (see Table 10.3). Five of them believed that their agreements would be renewed and expanded as older products were phased-out. New products would be launched before existing agreements ended. It was expected that the licensees follow the product policies of their licensers.

Table 10.3 Reasons for the renewal of technology transfer agreements by licensers

Reasons	Firms
Product phase-out	5
Licensees' inability to develop their own products	1
Marketing opportunities	1
Equity links	1
Total	8

One foreign firm argued that its Brazilian licensee did not have the necessary skills to develop new products in-house. Consequently, it would have to ask for another licence before phasing-out its current product line. Another foreign firm argued that market developments would determine the extension of licensing agreements. For another firm equity participation, which would give it a voice in the managerial decisions of their Brazilian licensee, was the reason for renewal of the agreement.

Three multinational firms did not see licensing agreements as lifelong relationships. One wished to start a larger-scale business in Brazil on a joint-venture basis which its current licensee did not wish to join. A second admitted that its Brazilian licensee had independently produced improvements in licensed products. Thus it would not want to renew the agreement. A third admitted that its licensee in Brazil had decided to follow its own path concerning product policy. In each case it was the Brazilian firm and not the licenser which had decided not to consider a renewal of the licensing agreements.

4 COMPETITION BETWEEN LICENSERS AND LICENSEES

The fear of future international competition influences multinationals' control and packaging strategies for licensing agreements. Multinational firms which licensed their technology to Brazil were asked if they feared that licensed firms, once they had access to their product and process design, might become international competitors. Three firms replied that they did. They had therefore imposed marketing limits on their Brazilian licensee. One licenser already in conflict with another licensee which had become a competitor in the European market, decided to adopt market restrictions in subsequent licensing agreements.

Most multinationals, however, said that they did not fear competition from their licensees. These firms had several advantages over their licensees (see Table 10.4).

Table 10.4 Licensers' perceptions of their relative competitive advantages *vis-à-vis* licensees

Competitive advantage	Firms
Lower price	6
Marketing support abroad	5
Better product	5
Not strong in export market	2
Total	18

Pricing

Lower costs reflected in lower export prices was the most frequently quoted competitive advantage of licensers. They produced on a larger scale than their licensees. This includes larger manufacturing plants and off-shore production of components. Also multinational corporations had preferential access to technology and sourcing of components.

The technology cost advantage of licensers derives from a larger scale of production which enables them to disperse R & D expenditure over a larger output. In addition, they enjoy returns from royalties. Table 10.5 shows R & D expenditure for licensers and licensees in three agreements in the Brazilian computer industry. All agreements stipulated royalty fees of 3 per cent of net sale price. But each company had a different method of charging for technical assistance and the provision of training. This may be merely the result of negotiation between the partners. From Table 10.5 we can see that the cost of technology for licensers is only about two-thirds of that for licensees.

Transfer pricing in the sale of components to licensees may also contribute to higher final prices of local manufactured products.

Table 10.5 Comparative technology costs for licensers and licensees 1979

Item	Licensee		Licenser	
	$1000	% total sales	$1000	% total sales
Case A				
R & D investment	3500	9.1	8500	5.3
Royalty payments	400	1.0	(400)	0.25
Net R & D investment	3900	10.1	8100	5.05
Difference		4.95		
Case B				
R & D investment	850	10.0	11 700	7.5
Royalty payments	100	1.25	(100)	0.06
Net R & D investment	950	11.25	11 600	7.44
Difference		3.81		
Case C				
R & D investment	1280	10.0	13 400	8.20
Royalty payments	150	1.2	(150)	0.09
Net R & D investment	1430	11.2	13 250	8.11
Difference		3.09		
Average				
R & D investment	–	9.7	–	7.00
Royalty payments	–	1.15	–	0.13
Net R & D investment	–	10.85	–	6.87
Difference		3.98		

Notes: R & D expenditure is estimated for data-processing equipment only. Licensers' royalty income does not include other licensing agreements.

Many local firms reported that all their imported components were supplied directly by the licenser. This gave the licenser an opportunity to overprice in a 'captive market'.

Indeed, two local firms claimed that their licensers were over-pricing. This took different forms. One firm reported that its licenser did not reduce the price of integrated circuits when they supplied them unassembled instead of assembled. The other claimed that the price charged for the supply of kits was higher than the final price of the assembled product in the licenser's home country.

The sale of kits and component parts is now more important, as a source of payment for technology transfer, than royalty payments. Eight out of nine licensers' firms reported that the sale of parts was their main form of return for technology transfer in the computer industry. Two of them said that royalties would become more important than the supply of goods in the long term.

Marketing

Most multinational firms have a well-established marketing network in other countries. This network includes marketing subsidiaries and distributors. Brazilian firms by contrast have virtually no marketing experience abroad. One licenser argued that it was no longer possible to find good computer distributors in developing countries because these have been taken up by American, European and Japanese firms.

The establishment of marketing facilities abroad, including service and distribution, is very costly and beyond the capacity of most Brazilian firms which are still involved with the development of a national marketing network.

Product differentiation

Five licensers claimed that they used product differentiation to prevent licensees competing in international markets. Two had introduced new models to substitute for the one they had licensed to Brazilian firms. Therefore, the products manufactured under licence in Brazil were no longer internationally competitive. The three other firms said they intended to launch new models in the near future which would not necessarily be included in licensing agreements.

11 CONCLUSIONS

The conclusions will review and discuss the evidence found in support of the hypotheses outlined in Part One.[1] It will also discuss the implications for policy.

1 COMPETITIVE ADVANTAGES OF MULTINATIONAL CORPORATIONS AND BARRIERS TO ENTRY

(Hyp. 1.1) Direct investment by multinational firms increases competition in national industry through the introduction of foreign technology to the local firms. (Hyp. 1.2) Direct investment by multinational firms in developing countries restrains competition and imposes oligopolistic barriers to entry for indigenous firms.

Studies of the effects of direct foreign investment by MNCs on competition in national industries have produced conflicting views. Conventional theories maintain that foreign investment contributes to the separation of efficient from inefficient firms in a process of 'natural selection'. Behrman (1970) argued that

Direct investment usually goes into the technically advanced industries, adding to the competitiveness of the host industry and its ability to export or meet foreign competition.

Johnson too (1970) emphasized the benefits for the receiving economy derived from the superior efficiency of foreign firms.

An alternative view is taken by Stephen Hymer (1972). He found that direct foreign investment was an instrument for restraining competition. Therefore restrictions on direct investment or a policy of breaking up a multinational corporation may in some cases be the only way of establishing a higher degree of competition in that industry. Similarly, Newfarmer (1979b) argued that foreign direct investment was closely linked with monopolization and the erection of barriers to entry. He believed that

[1] Where reference is made to findings to a percentage of firms, this will refer to a percentage of the firms interviewed with respect to the relevant issue for that particular section of the conclusion.

Barriers to entry which protect the monopolistic advantages of MNCs are not solely based on superior technology, but include corporate practices designed to deter new entry.

This study of the Brazilian computer industry found that the competitive behaviour of local subsidiaries of MNCs creates barriers to entry for indigenous firms. This is because of the importance of goodwill and brand names in the market for data-processing equipment and because of the absolute competitive advantages enjoyed by MNCs.

Goodwill and brand names play important roles in product selection as the choice of computers is not made on a purely rational basis. Customers cannot accurately evaluate the performance of the machines due to different functions and configurations presented by different computers (e.g. operational system, processing speed and input/output capabilities). They tend to prefer products manufactured by international companies which enjoy goodwill. A computer bureau manager, for example, reported that there were three brands of computer terminals installed in his centre—IBM, Scopus, and Cobra. Although the machines performed identically the operators preferred IBM terminals.

Competition in the computer business favours current suppliers. It is difficult for users to replace an entire system once it is installed. Therefore users are generally unwilling to change brands unless absolutely compelled to. Switching computer suppliers may require the re-writing of programs due to incompatibility of operational systems and basic software. It may also involve the retraining of personnel and a change in customers' systems and methods. Consequently, companies which had been in the Brazilian market for a long time were found to enjoy an advantage over new suppliers with a similar annual turnover but a smaller number of installations in that country.

This study found that MNCs have absolute cost advantages vis-à-vis Brazilian minicomputer manufacturers. This was due to three factors. First, MNCs pay relatively less than local firms to obtain access to technology, since they enjoy economies of scale in R & D and technology transfer. Second, MNCs enjoy economies of scale from world-wide operations. IBM do Brazil, for example, has a large volume of trade with other overseas subsidiaries of the corporation. This enables a volume of production and economies of scale larger than the size of the local market would permit. Third, MNCs enjoy lower cost of finance. In 1979, for example, IBM raised two blocks of soft loans on the US capital market totalling

$2.5 billion.[2] The company used these to meet capital requirements for the construction of manufacturing plants and for rental equipment. The loans obtained by IBM were larger than the value of the sales of all Brazilian computer manufacturers combined in the period 1979–81.

Large capital and profit resulting from scale benefits have enabled IBM to undertake competitive strategies such as discriminatory pricing which have forced other successful but smaller companies to avoid direct competition with it. As John Cunningan, executive vice-president of Wang Laboratories, a pacesetter in the market for smaller computers said:

We have survived as a company because we respect IBM. We have always made sure that when they move we got out of the way, so that we got hit only by a glancing blow on the side, instead of a crushing blow to the head.

(*FT*, 18 March 1981.)

The market dominance and monopolistic practices of IBM have been the subject of several legal inquiries in Europe and the USA. In January 1982 the US Dept. of Justice dropped its 13-year anti-trust case against IBM. But the computer giant still faces private anti-trust cases in the USA and an action by the European Commission, which has complained against IBM's business practices in the EEC.[3]

Backward and forward vertical integration in the computer market can create barriers to entry not only in the mainframe market but also in peripherals, components and software services. Multinational computer firms can utilize their control over the mainframe market to keep control over the market for terminals, tape and disk drives and printers. This is achieved by the introduction of unique software (e.g. secret protocol) and hardware (e.g. special semiconductor devices) which render mainframe computers incompatible with peripherals produced by independent plug-compatible manufacturers. Because a large share of the computers installed in Brazil are IBM, the company holds about 70 per cent of the Brazilian market for VDUs. Three local manufacturers—Cobra, Embracomp and Scopus —developed IBM-compatible VDUs. These are linked to IBM computers via modem by the Binary Synchronous Code (BSC) protocol.

[2] The company arranged a $1.5 billion credit line with a group of 37 banks. Only eight weeks later IBM announced a $1 billion bond offering consisting of $500 million in notes due in 1986 and $500 million of debentures due in 2009. It was believed to be the largest single public corporate debt offering in the USA since American Telephone and Telegraph raised $1.5 billion in 1970 (*FT*, September 1973).

[3] In November 1981 the European Court of Justice in Luxemburg ruled against IBM's application for the annulment of the EEC's decisions to begin proceedings on IBM's competitive practices in Europe (*Computer Weekly*, 19 November 1981, p. 1.)

IBM blocked attempted competition in that market by introducing a new control unit (370X) which requires a protocol (SDLC) only available in its own terminals.

Leading computer MNCs are also substantially vertically integrated into components. When IBM introduced its first commercial electronic computer in 1953, all its vacuum tubes were purchased from outside suppliers. The company adopted a policy of producing all key components in-house. Ten years later the entire 360 line was designed around a hybrid circuit called Solid Logic Technology (SLT) produced in-house by IBM's component division. Although in the 1970s and 1980s the company had increased its reliance on outside semiconductor suppliers which had introduced other faster and denser devices, it still produces a major proportion of semiconductors in-house. The new technology utilized in very large scale integrated circuits (VLSI) may be making the design of the semiconductor an integral part of the design of the computers themselves. This can increase market concentration and pose competitive challenges to both independent manufacturers and to computer makers without in-house semiconductor capabilities.

Computers require a wide range of technical services aimed at ensuring the efficient use of the equipment. This includes technical maintenance and support for the development of application software.

When all these services are provided by the DP equipment manufacturer itself, there is forward vertical integration. Alternatively, such services could be provided by end-users themselves or by independent firms. The Brazilian computer industry includes each of these types of arrangements. Embracomp, for example, provides maintenance services for its customers through an independent technicians' co-operative. Brazilian micro and minicomputer manufacturers are increasingly contracting independent software houses to obtain additional help in developing application software (see Table 6.12). But multinational computer companies tend to dominate those segments by offering a package including the equipment, maintenance and software on a monthly or yearly lease basis. This has important monopolistic consequences of creating barriers to entry for independent systems and software houses and maintenance service firms.

The oligopolistic barriers to entry created by MNCs for indigenous computer firms have important policy implications which are examined at the end of this chapter.

2   OWNERSHIP STRATEGY AND TECHNOLOGY TRANSFER

(Hyp. 2.1) Majority local partnership in overseas subsidiaries permits local control over policies and operations. This enables technology transfer through access to technical knowledge generated abroad.

(Hyp. 2.2) Even majority local partnership in overseas subsidiaries of MNCs does not necessarily confer local control over policies and operations or technology transfer.

Policies of ownership and control of overseas subsidiaries by multinational corporations

This study found that MNCs with unique strength in product and process design, marketing and management, and with sufficient financial resources to enter overseas markets preferred total ownership of subsidiaries. The performance for such strategies was related with the product line the subsidiary was involved in. Some companies had particular strength in some product lines but did not have it in others. If a firm had no unique strength in a particular product line it was more likely to accept a partner who could provide the necessary additional technical or managerial help. This was also likely when the proposed activity was secondary to the main interest of the parent company.

IBM has always firmly refused to enter into any joint venture in the computer business—a field in which the company has outstanding competitive advantages world-wide. In India in 1977 IBM refused to offer locals equity as the government wanted. The company withdrew from the country rather than comply. IBM accepted, however, to enter into joint ventures in areas in which it had no previous expertise. It did so with SBS for satellites and with MCA for the development and marketing of video-disk equipment.

Sixteen out of the 21 foreign multinationals in the Brazilian computer industry perceived themselves to have unique strength. They preferred to operate wholly owned subsidiaries (see Table 9.6). Reasons of competitive security were given by the firms who preferred absolute control over the operations of their subsidiaries. Computer manufacture requires continuous flow of information to affiliates in the firm. This is made particularly necessary when local plants concentrate on test and assembly only, and rely on the overseas parents for components and technical inputs such as basic electronics, software and R & D. Large computer multinationals developed a strong competitive position globally, based on their oligopolistic competitive advantages. They maintain strict world-wide control over products, marketing and managerial policies to preserve these advantages.

This study found that although MNCs prefer wholly owned foreign subsidiaries, policy regulations often compel them to accept local partners. Firms' ownership strategies were thus directly influenced by the policies of host governments. But even though most computer MNCs in Brazil would have no choice other than to give up a controlling share of their subsidiaries' equity if this were required by the computer authorities, it would not necessarily result in loss of control by the parents over important functions such as product policy and technological decisions. The director of a large US computer firm said that his firm would accept a joint-venture arrangement in Brazil only if forced by the government, but the local partners would only be a 'front'. MNCs adopt several means to prevent real devolution of control to their partly owned subsidiaries. These include care in the terms upon which they are prepared to enter into technology exchange and care in the selection of their local partners. One European firm reported that a detailed business plan is arranged with foreign partners before any joint-venture arrangement is concluded. This involves unambiguous demarcation of responsibilities over strategic issues such as product policy, technical and managerial decisions between the partners.

Olivetti is another example of means by which extensive ownership did not reflect actual management control. Olivetti announced plans to 'nationalize' its local subsidiary by selling shares on the local stock exchange (Dados v. 5, no. 2, 1980), after having several minicomputer manufacturing plans turned down by the SEI on the grounds that this segment of the computer market was reserved for Brazilian-owned firms. Local shareholders, however, would typically be too dispersed to provide an effective voice in management and Olivetti's management control would not be dissipated.

MNCs maintain management or technical control when the local investors are financial institutions or firms belonging to different industrial sectors.[4] Local investors may exercise some control over profits but will have little willingness or capability to become involved in technical decisions. This may have occurred with Telematica, a mainframe computer manufacturer 40 per cent owned by CII-Honeywell Bull and 60 per cent by the Brazilian holding company

[4] The Japanese government have always recognized the uselessness of this kind of arrangement for technology-transfer purposes. It encouraged joint ventures between local and foreign companies only when the firms belonged to the same industrial sector. Only then may the local firm have the opportunity to acquire technical capacity to learn and influence the technology introduced by their partners (Tigre, 1978).

Unipec. Unipec is owned by two groups lacking previous experience in computer manufacturing—Brazilinvest, a venture capital firm, and Pereira Lopez, a white goods manufacturer. Despite its majority share the Brazilian group has clearly a subordinate role with respect to technological decisions.

Joint ventures and technology transfer

Only one out of 14 Brazilian DP equipment manufacturers considered that technology transfer would be improved through joint ventures with the licenser. The majority considered that existing licensing agreements provided sufficient know-how to manufacture computer products locally. In fact they feared that joint venture with foreign firms would actually result in a loss of autonomy in technical and some strategic economic decisions.

In product areas where the firms had no technical know-how they had no autonomy to lose. Firms in this situation were prepared to enter into joint ventures. The majority of joint ventures under such conditions resulted in technology dependence of the local firm.

This study found that joint ventures did not favour technology transfer when the foreign partner took responsibility for co-ordinating technical decisions. For several reasons, foreign partners were not interested in reducing dependence on imported technology. First, local technology autonomy could create conflicts with the optimization of the corporation product policy world-wide. Second, supply of technology usually means the supply of kits and components. If the local firm designs its products autonomously, it may find alternative sources of supply of components locally or abroad and thus reduce imports from its foreign partner. Third, local dependence on a foreign partner's technology is a guarantee against an effective local take-over.

Typically, foreign partners were unwilling to introduce schemes which genuinely trained local personnel to undertake product and process design activities. Local enterprises were induced to restrict R & D on the ground of duplication of innovation expenses already incurred elsewhere by the parent company. This study found that all the foreign computer firms were pressuring the Brazilian partly owned firms to reject the development of new products and only to manufacture products already developed by the corporation abroad.

Coensisa is a Brazilian modem manufacturer partly owned (40 per cent) by Racal Milgo—a Miami-based subsidiary of Racal Electronics (UK). In March 1981 Racal negotiated an investment plan with its Brazilian partner involving the following conditions:

Coencisa should manufacture only communication equipment developed by Racal Milgo or equipment already produced by other subsidiaries of the Racal Group such as Vadic and Tacticom.
Coencisa should drastically reduce its R & D activities.
Coencisa should only manufacture equipment which utilize the latest available technology.

The Brazilian partner refused these conditions on the grounds that the products which offered the best sales potential were those designed and developed in Brazil. According to the general director of Coencisa, these did not incorporate the latest available technology nor did they depend on imported components. Consequently, they were competitive in price not only in Brazil, but also in other Latin American countries. Coencisa was able to turn down Racal's proposal because of the availability of an alternative local source of financial help.[5]

3 STRATEGIES OF MULTINATIONALS CONCERNING THE SALE OF TECHNOLOGY

(Hyp. 3.1) Licenser firms prefer to offer a 'package' of equity-investment managerial skills and technical knowledge rather than to simply license their know-how.

(Hyp. 3.2) In recent years licensers have shifted their preference from equity investment and management control to the sale of technology and management services.

Studies on whether MNCs prefer to link the sale of technology to equity shares have produced conflicting findings. Hymer (1960) found that in order to preserve their oligopolistic competitive advantages MNCs avoided selling their technology unless it was linked to investment. Monopoly over technological assets embodied in product design or know-how would be jeopardized if MNCs sell these to potential competitors who currently lack them. Similarly, Caves (1971) found that in order to maximize their profits, MNCs must tie their knowledge to direct control over the process of production and distribution.

However, Baranson (1978) found that evolutionary trends in the world economy have changed corporate viewpoints about direct involvement and management of their technological assets abroad. Consequently, a growing number of corporations were adopting

---

[5] The 'Banco Regional de Brasilia' agreed to invest US $1 million in Coencisa which would be utilized to pay Coencisa's debt to Racal Milgo. (*Datanews*, 18 March 1981.)

an explicit policy of shifting from equity investment and managerial control of overseas facilities to the direct sale of technology and management services purely as a means of earning returns on corporate assets.

The findings of this study reveal that the strategies adopted by computer MNCs for the sale of technology varied according to firms' relative size and competitive strength. The correlation between very large firms and the adoption of wholly owned strategies in Brazil was strongly positive (Q = 0.826, see Figure 9.1). 'Centralized multinationals' have been defined in Chapter 9 as those firms which adopted strict control policies in relation to marketing, product, manufacturing and procurement world-wide. Correlation between centralized multinationals and the adoption of wholly owned ownership strategies was Q = 1.

Assessment of firms ownership *preferences* as opposed to what they *actually did*, reveal that it was not only large firms which preferred to link the sale of technology to direct foreign investment. Medium-size firms also showed preferences for ownership over firms abroad receiving their technology, rather than just licensing their knowledge to third parties. Of the 21 MNCs studied only three indicated simply licensing technology as their first preference in exploiting overseas markets.

Despite widespread *preference* for linking the sale of technology to equity investment, only very large computer firms could afford to pursue this strategy effectively in Brazil. Eleven out of 15 medium-to-large MNCs felt compelled to sell computer technology without any equity or managerial involvement (see Table 9.1). Being smaller, they were more susceptible than larger multinationals to the demands of Brazilian computer authorities for technology sharing. Also they faced competition from other enterprises as suppliers of computer technology to Brazil and were under pressure to release technology early in the product cycle. For example, in 1979 the Brazilian firm Flexidisk tried to obtain a license from Shugart[6] to manufacture floppy-disk drives in Brazil. Shugart refused on the grounds that its corporate policy was not to sell newly developed technology. Later, however, when Flexidisk was on the brink of signing a technology transfer agreement with another American manufacturer (Pertec), Shugart realized that its policy could cause it to lose the fast-growing Brazilian market. Thus it changed its policy and agreed to license floppy-disk drives to Flexidisk. In order to

[6] Shugart Associates is a subsidiary of the Xerox Corporation. It holds 60 per cent of the American market of 5-inch floppy-disk drives.

regain the deal Shugart went as far as to offer better price conditions than Pertec.[7]

Smaller multinationals usually had inadequate financial and managerial resources to get involved in overseas manufacturing to compete with the larger multinationals in permitted segments of the Brazilian market.

Some smaller companies like Logabax and Data Products admitted that they had a passive role in the licensing business in Brazil. They had opportunities to sell data-processing technology to that country and could not consider alternatives such as direct foreign investment. Some large technology suppliers such as Ampex, Fujitsu and Control Data had insisted in taking equity shares in their licensees. But since Brazilian firms, for political reasons, preferred pure licensing agreements, these suppliers accepted just licensing their know-how.

DEC, the world's largest minicomputer manufacturer,[8] had been involved in licensing negotiations with Cobra in the early 1970s. But the agreement did not come into effect because the US firm insisted on taking a majority share in the Brazilian computer company. In 1976 Data General, the second largest independent minicomputer manufacturer in the world,[9] also started to negotiate a licensing agreement with Cobra for its Nova technology. The negotiations broke down because DG refused to transfer its technology ownership to Cobra at the end of the agreement. The international leaders in the minicomputer business chose to wait for policy changes permitting wholly owned manufacturing subsidiaries before making large-scale entry to the Brazilian market. As one manager remarked: 'We will be here long after this government has passed on; the next may see it our way.'

Control Data is a rare example of an international market leader which did opt to go overseas through joint ventures and licensing agreements. CDC is the world's largest manufacturer of computer peripheral devices. It selected this strategy in order to compete with IBM whose sales of computer products were about eight times as large ($22 billion versus $2.7 billion in 1980). In Brazil CDC supplies technology for manufacturing disk drives purely on a licensing basis.

[7] Shugart charged a lump sum of $70,000 for the transfer of technology against $725,000 fixed by Pertec. In addition, the unitary price of Shugart's 8 inch floppy-disk drives to be supplied to Flexidisk was fixed at $345 against $475 for Pertec's.

[8] In 1980 DEC's total sales was $2.7 billion. The company operates overseas through seven wholly owned manufacturing plants and has marketing subsidiaries in 38 countries.

[9] In 1980 Data General's total sales were $673 million. All DG computers are manufactured in the USA for export, although a manufacturing licence was granted to a Japanese firm in 1972 for the manufacture and sale of some company products in Japan.

4   LICENSING AGREEMENTS, COMPETITION AND
    TECHNOLOGY TRANSFER

This section will explore the hypothesis concerning licensing agreements. This includes conclusions about the reasons for undertaking licensing agreements and their implications for technology dependence and exports.

Reasons for undertaking licensing agreements

It has been hypothesized that licensing is necessary because of:
The complexity of technology (Hyp. 4.1).
The competitive environment (Hyp. 4.2).
The cost advantage and risks of own product development (Hyp. 4.3).
The advantages of gaining access to particular brand names and by previous relationships with licensers (Hyp. 4.4).

Decisions by developing countries firms to buy foreign technology have been traditionally attributed to two major factors: first is the lack of indigenous technical capabilities with design and develop products and process in-house. Second is the higher cost of developing technology in-house compared to the lower cost of obtaining it through licensing agreements with foreign firms.

Recent empirical studies, however, have shown this may not be so.[10] The findings of this study on the Brazilian computer industry also largely rejects the traditional explanation. Sixty per cent of the firms interviewed argued that they entered licensing agreements either because competitors did so or because the time required for in-house product development was too long (see Table 7.8). Most of these firms mentioned that there were technical capabilities either within the firm or in local universities to develop alternatives to products licensed from foreign firms. However, firms chose licensing because they faced direct competition from licensed products which were already proven and enjoyed goodwill in the local market. There was scepticism among these firms about the

---

[10] In his study of 123 Argentinian firms, Sercovich (1975) found that the major reason for licensing was that it permitted national firms to enter oligopolistic markets in which competition was structured by the standards set through foreign imports. Mytelka (1978) studied the reasons for undertaking licensing agreements of metalworking and chemical firms located in Peru, Ecuador and Colombia. More than half of the firms interviewed gave 'brand name' considerations as one of the reasons for licensing, thus implying entry into a 'quality segment' of the market in which standards had been set by foreign imports.

competitiveness of locally designed products in the face of market standards already set by foreign technology.

In apparent support to traditional theories, complexity of the technology was the second most-quoted reason for Brazilian DP equipment manufacturers undertaking licensing agreements. Forty per cent of the firms interviewed mentioned that the technology involved in licensed products was complex and that external help was needed in order to begin manufacturing activities. However, two-thirds of the firms which mentioned complexity of technology as one of the reasons for undertaking licensing were in the business of manufacturing printers or tape drives, which require high-precision mechanical technology, a field in which there were few skilled professionals available locally. But for data-processing equipment such as microcomputers, modems and terminals which relies on electronic rather than mechanical technology, complexity of technology played a minor role in Brazilian firms' decision to enter into licensing agreements.

The third most cited reason for entering into licensing was the risk involved in undertaking product development in-house. This was mentioned by 27 per cent of the firms interviewed. The risks concerned uncertainties about price, quality standards and market conditions. Firms minimize the risks when they gain access to an already tested technology through licensing agreements.

Brand name considerations were quoted by only 13.5 per cent of the firms interviewed. Since DP equipment manufactured in Brazil does not show licenser's brand names, the goodwill enjoyed by known trade marks played a secondary role in firms' decision to enter into licensing agreements. 'Previous relationships with licensers' also played a minor role in licensing since most firms have had no previous commercial or technological links with their licensers.

The main conclusion to be drawn from this analysis of technology sourcing is that 'market factors' such as product competition and speed of market entry are more important than 'technological factors' in Brazilian DP equipment firms' decisions to undertake licensing agreements.

Implications for control of local firms

Licensing agreements may have important implications for licensees' freedom concerning marketing, product strategy, production, technology development and procurement policy. The mechanisms adopted by technology suppliers to keep control over such decisions in licensed firms have been studied by a number of economists in recent years. These studies include those by Vaitsos (1971), Sercovich (1975), Penrose (1976), Cooper and Maxwell (1975) and Mytelka (1978) and they concluded that licensing agreements may constrain licensees' autonomy concerning basic and strategic decisions.

The findings of this study are that licensing agreements between Brazilian and foreign firms do not result in significant dependence in basic decisions such as capital raising and expenditure, dividend policy and organizational policy. However, for logistic and strategic decisions the evidence suggests that in many cases licensers' influence is significant. These areas include licensee's marketing, product strategy, and procurement policy.

Some licensees nevertheless retain a considerable degree of freedom concerning logistic and strategic decisions. Generally, favourability of the terms of technology transfer depends on the relative bargaining power of the two parties. Only three out of 18 foreign firms which sold DP equipment to Brazilian companies were very large firms (see Table 9.8). Thus, most technology suppliers had insufficient economic power to exercise strict control over their licensees. They lacked the resources to insist upon arrangements including a package of management, finance and technology.

However, preference for packages was not only a supplier-determined phenomena. If the technology receiver lacked the technical or financial capabilities to invest significantly in R & D the receiver itself will often prefer a packaged transfer agreement.

Government regulations played an important role in restricting agreements involving packaging and control. Brazilian regulations concerning technology transfer agreements (Ato Normativo, no. 15 —INPI) explicitly ban most types of restrictive clauses in licensing agreements. Also the government bodies in charge of computer policy in Brazil have attempted to exclude packaging and restrictive operations by advising local firms in negotiations with foreign technology suppliers, and by themselves refusing permission for projects involving control by licensers.

However, product policy, including product changes and competition, is widely used by licensers as an instrument to restrict licensees' managerial and technical independence. Product changes involving replacement of key components may lead to the discontinuation of a licensed product. If there are no alternative suppliers for the new components the licensee will be compelled to follow its licenser's product change. For example, Edisa continues to manufacture a minicomputer model under licence from Fujitsu which has been phased out in Japan. Fujitsu still supplies kits and components for Edisa, but it is pressuring the Brazilian firm to discontinue the product on the grounds that it is no longer profitable to Fujitsu to supply the components for Brazil only.

In each segment of the Brazilian DP equipment industry there are three or four indigenous firms which operate a manufacturing licence from a major foreign manufacturer. Permanent product policy links of local firms with foreign technology suppliers were discouraged through government requirements permitting licensing agreements only to establish initial product lines. Modifications to products were to be developed locally. But even if one local firm introduces a product innovation from its foreign licensers, local competitors have little alternative but quickly to follow suit. The long-term consequence of this competitive process is that local firms lack incentive to invest in product innovation in the face of technological comparative advantage of licensers.

Implication for exports

The findings of this study are that computer products manufactured under licence to foreign firms have very poor chances for export success. Only 8 per cent of the licensed firms considered that they had good export prospects compared with nearly 55 per cent for firms which developed their products in-house.

There are two main factors explaining the likely poor export performance of licensed products. First, despite government regulations against it, most licensed products face export restrictions. These are in the form of unwritten agreements between partners and include export prohibitions to specific countries, a ban on all exports, authorization to export only to the licenser itself and bans on selling abroad on an OEM basis. Licensers usually guarantee their control over licensees' export activities through control of the production and shipping of important components which are supplied to Brazil. This power is exercised, for example, through the threat to deny future supply of components if the licensee unilaterally takes the decision to export.

The second factor is the competitive advantages of licensers *vis-à-vis* licensees. These include lower cost enabling power price, better marketing support abroad and better product design. Licensers are able to offer better export prices than their licensees for three reasons. First, they produce on a larger scale which enables the realization of economies of scale in manufacturing and marketing. Cheap off-shore production of components and assembly provide further cost advantages for some firms. Second, the cost of technology for licensers (measured on a per unit product basis) has been shown to be significantly lower than the cost of the same technology for the licensees (see Table 10.5).

A third reason is price discrimination in the sale of components to licensees. This study found at least two cases of local firms which were being overpriced in the supply of kits and components (see p. 155).

There is a large competitive differential in the extent of marketing support abroad between licensers and their Brazilian licensees. Licensers are usually MNCs with well-established marketing networks in other countries. Brazilian firms, by contrast, have little marketing experience abroad and lack financial resources to break into and establish their own marketing facilities in other countries.

The export prospects of computer products manufactured in Brazil under licence to foreign firms are also constrained by obsolete product design. Three licensers claimed that they had already introduced new models which were more competitive than the products they had just licensed to Brazil. The international competitiveness of the products manufactured in Brazil was diminished. Three other MNCs were at the point of launching new products whose design would not necessarily be transferred to their licensees.

Export from Brazilian subsidiaries of large multinationals such as IBM, Burroughs and CII-Honeywell Bull constitute a special case. Typically their export performance is a result of the policy of the corporation as a whole determined at Corporate Headquarters. IBM, for example, exports about two-thirds of total production of the locally assembled 4300 line to other countries.

Brazilian firms engaged in the export business are in direct competition with large multinationals. The Brazilian firms main competitive advantage is original product design, rather than price or marketing services. At least three local firms—Cobra, Polymax and Racimec—had already started to export on a regular basis. In 1981 Polymax concluded an export deal for the supply of 1000 locally designed microcomputers to China. Since China was interested in developing its own computer industry, the deal included a commitment to technology transfer. Polymax is now concentrating its efforts on Latin America and has already arranged independent distributors in several countries. In 1982 Racimec sold 6000 football pools terminals worth more than $20 million to Argentina and Chile.

5   POLICY IMPLICATIONS

This section will assess the main implications of the hypothesis examined in this work for state policies designed to encourage the development of an independent computer industry in Brazil.

A major problem to industrial policy has been identified in this study. New firms in developing countries, or even other developed countries firms, may not be able to enter the local market successfully in the absence of government measures limiting the effects of the dominance of MNCs in these markets. The findings of this study supported (Hyp. 1.2) that direct investment by MNCs in developing countries restrains competition and imposes oligopolistic barriers to entry for indigenous firms. This is of particular significance for technologically advanced industrial sectors such as the computer industry.

The computer industry is an example of activity which offers considerable opportunities for independent industrial and technological development to countries which have reached a certain level of scientific and market development. As Pickering (1974) claimed:

> In technologically-oriented industries, new entry is most likely to occur at times when a major new innovation has just arisen. This is the time at which knowledge barriers are lowest and entrant firms are at less of a disadvantage than they would be at other periods of time when there is a static technology and when substantial learning effects have already been achieved by existing firms.

However, once market segments have been open to MNCs, local firms are not able to overcome the oligopolistic barriers to entry. Some developed countries like Japan recognized the need to protect some segments of their industry against international competition. At the beginning of the 1970s Japanese industry was already at a mature stage—but it still needed protection from direct competition with large foreign MNCs. As Yoshiro (1970) stated:

> Japanese industries have shown tremendous growth since the war; but they are still on the whole too weak and vulnerable to be exposed to the full rigor of competition from giant MNCs.

At this time, according to Dosi (1980), protection of the Japanese electronic industry included: (a) very restrictive regulations on foreign investment, (b) institutional definitions and public monitoring of the terms of licensing agreements, (c) import control and (d) setting of 'technological targets' and establishment of adequate research facilities to fulfil them.

Protected from imports and local manufacture by MNCs, Brazilian computer firms have successfully entered the market. They now supply to local customers a wide range of licensed and locally designed products. Despite sometimes higher prices than those in the developed countries, products are more appropriate to the local needs because they are designed to match local requirements for users applications, quality, and performance. Bank terminals, for example, have been especially designed to suit the characteristics of the Brazilian banking system. Most customers perceive the advantages of having a local computer industry. The Brazilian Society of Computer Users (Sucesu), for example, has given support for the development of an indigenous computer industry on the grounds that it would benefit customers in the medium and long term. However, if protection were lifted, MNCs would regain market dominance through aggressive marketing, pricing and product strategies, and the matching of computer products to local needs could no longer be guaranteed.

One of the major foundations of computer policy in Brazil has been discrimination between local and foreign-owned firms. This would become difficult if subsidiaries of MNCs were disguised behind a 'façade' of being locally owned. The findings supported the hypothesis (Hyp. 2.2) that even majority local partnership in overseas subsidiaries of MNCs does not necessarily enable local control over policies and operations or technology transfer.

Joint ventures between local and foreign computer firms have not been encouraged by either Capre or SEI. But many computer MNCs have plans to 'nationalize' their Brazilian subsidiaries in order to overcome the 'market reserve policy' by introducing actual control by MNCs behind a façade of local ownership.

The introduction of foreign capital to locally owned firms has similar implications. Many local firms could be tempted to accept financial help from their licensers in order to overcome the inadequacy of domestic capital markets. This may be particularly so for firms which have financially strong licensers such as Fujitsu, Nixdorf and Control Data. This can further hinder local technological development because these firms would acquire the means to influence the Brazilian licensees to adopt a more dependent technological strategy.

When the foreign firms undertake portfolio investment—often with small shares of several local firms—the danger of losing autonomy is less serious. Foreign financial firms or venture capital companies, for example, are usually primarily concerned with the overall short-term financial performance of the firms rather than with becoming involved with technological decisions. They may prefer to allow the firm to pursue strategies of technology independence as long as they obtain an acceptable return on investment.

The strategies of MNCs concerning the sale of technology (Hyp. 3.1 and Hyp. 3.2) have also important policy implications. National policies designed to promote technology transfer through pure licensing agreements between local and foreign-owned firms, cannot achieve their objectives through reliance on international market leaders or 'centralized multinationals'. It was found that the corporate strategies in exploiting their technology abroad operates in two distinct ways: one pattern for the 'centralized MNCs', which exercised strict control over both basic and strategic decisions, and another for the 'decentralized firms' which adopted loose control over one or more important basic and logistic decisions. Local firms should be encouraged therefore to concentrate their negotiating efforts on medium-sized or 'decentralized' foreign companies, which are much more likely to release technology without insisting on equity partnership.

Only if government objectives are simply to attract large amounts of foreign direct investment rather than to stimulate the development of technological capabilities should it seek to attract large or 'centralized' multinationals. Such firms do offer the advantage of being able to respond quickly to incentives for local DP equipment assembly or manufacturing.

Even when technical capabilities to design and develop specific products are available locally, externally induced market forces often compel local firms to enter licensing agreements. It was found that the main reason for undertaking licensing was the competitive environment (Hyp. 4.1). If the goal of local technological development is to be attained, the government must intervene. Several avenues are open to government. By restraining the inflow of foreign technology while local firms develop alternative products in-house or by enabling the import of key know-how or components only, the government will induce local firms to design products locally.

This was well illustrated by SEI's decision in March 1982 not to allow licensing agreements to obtain the newly developed Winchester technology for disk drives. Firms were encouraged to design the equipment in-house and then to seek for independent foreign manufacturers for the supply of key components such as, magnetic recording heads and integrated circuits. By so doing, firms developed their own design capabilities without dependence on a single technology or component supplier. Firms felt secure to pursue this strategy as competitors were not allowed to take short-cuts importing complete products under licensing agreements with foreign manufacturers.

This study found that data-processing equipment manufactured under licence to foreign firms has poor export prospects. The success of a state export policy will depend, to a large extent, on indigenous industry capacity to design and develop original products in-house. The export performance of manufacturing subsidiaries of MNCs is influenced by government policies, costs and corporate policy. IBM and Burroughs, for example, accepted SEI's demand to export more than half of their computer production in return for permission to sell large computers in Brazil.

State policy initiatives have been shown to substantially contribute towards the development of a more internationally competitive indigenous computer industry in Brazil. The success of Capre and SEI suggests that, at least with respect to exports, intelligent and aggressive state policies can extract some benefits from MNCs for the local industry which may not be obtained in its absence.

Bibliography

Adam, G., 'Multinational Corporations and Worldwide Sourcing', Radice, H. (ed.), *International Firms and Modern Imperialism*, Penguin Modern Economics Reading, 1975.

Adams, Walter (ed.), *The Structure of American Industry*, Macmillan, 1977.

Ady, Peter (ed.), *Private Foreign Investment and the Developing World*, Praeger, New York, 1971.

Ajami, Fouad, 'Corporate Giants—Some Global Social Costs', Modelski, G. (ed.), *Transnational Corporations and World Order*, W. H. Freeman and Company, San Francisco, 1979.

Alejandro, C. D. 'Direct Foreign Investment in Latin America', Kindleberger, C. (ed.), *The International Corporation*, MIT Press, Cambridge, Mass., 1970.

Aliber, R. Z., 'A Theory of Direct Investment', Kindleberger, C., *The International Corporation*, MIT Press, Cambridge, Mass., 1970.

Alsegg, Robert J., *Control Relationships Between American Corporations and their European Subsidiaries*, American Management Association, New York, 1971.

Amin, Samin, *Imperialism and Unequal Development*, Harvester Press, 1978.

Ansoff, I., 'Strategy for a Technology-based Business', *Harvard Business Review, R & D Management Series*, vol. 2, November/December 1967.

Ansoff, I., *Corporate Strategy*, McGraw-Hill, 1965; Pelican, 1970.

Arrow, K. J., 'The Economic Implications of Learning by Doing', *Review of Economic Studies*, no. 29, June 1962.

Bain, J., *Barriers to New Competition*, Harvard University Press, Cambridge, Mass., 1956, 1967.

Baker, M. (ed.), *Industrial Innovation, Technology, Policy Diffusion*, Macmillan, 1979.

Baran, P. and Sweezy, P., *Monopoly Capital—An Essay on the American Economic and Social Order*, Penguin, 1966, 1977.

Baranson, J., 'Technology Transfer through the International Firm', *American Economic Review*, 1970.

Baranson, J., *Technology and the Multinationals*, Lexington Books, 1978.

Barnet, R. and Muller, R. *Global Reach*, Cape, London, 1975.

Behrman, J., *National Interests and the Multinational Enterprise*, Prentice-Hall, 1970.

Behrman, J. and Wallender, H., *Transfer of Manufacturing Technology within Multinational Enterprises*, Ballinger Publishing Company, Cambridge, Mass., 1976.

Bennett, R., 'IBM in Latin America', in Gunnemann, J. (ed.), *The Nation, State and Transnational Corporations in Conflict*, Praeger, New York, 1975.

Biato, F. e Figueiredo, M., *A Transferencia de Tecnologia no Brasil*, IPEA, Serie Estudos para o Planejamento, no. 4, Brasilia, 1973.

Bienefeld, M., 'Dependency in the Eighties', in *IDS Bulletin*, December 1980, vol. 12, no. 1.

Biondi, A., 'O preco invisivel da tecnologia importada', *Dados e Ideias*, vol. 1, no. 1, August/September, 1975.

Blalock, H., *Social Statistics*, International Student Edition, McGraw-Hill, 1960, 1972.

Bradbury, F. R., *'Business Machines' IBM Corporation*, Stirling Forum on Technology Transfer, December 1976, mimeo.

Brandt, W. and Hulbert, J., *Managing the Multinational Subsidiary in Brazil; A Preliminary Summary to Participating Managers*, Graduate School of Business, Columbia University, 1974.

Brandt, W. and Hulbert, J., *A Empresa Multinational no Brasil*, Zahar Editors, 1977.

Brash, D. T., *American Investment in Australian Industry*, Harvard University Press, Cambridge, 1969.

Bridge, J., *Planning and the Growth of the Firm*, Croom Helm, 1978.

Britton, J. and Guilmour, J., *The Weakest Link. A Technological Perspective on Canadian Industrial Underdevelopment*, Science Council of Canada, Ottawa, 1978.

Brock, G., *The US Computer Industry 1954-1973: A Study of Market Power*, Ballinger Publishing Company, Cambridge, Mass., 1975.

Brooke, M. and Rammers, H., *The Strategy of Multinational Enterprise—Organisation and Finance*, Longman, 1970.

Brown, M., 'Some International Issues in the Development of Local Engineering Capabilities', *OECD Development Centre, Industry and Technology Occasional Paper, No. 28*, July 1978.

Brown, M. B., *The Economics of Imperialism*, Penguin Modern Economics Texts, 1974.

Business Week, *Survey in Sales and Profits*, McGraw-Hill, March 1976, 1977, 1978, 1979, 1980 and 1981.

Business Week, *Annual Survey in R & D Spending by US Firms*, McGraw-Hill, June 1976, 1979, 1980.

Canada, Science Council, *Strategies of Development for the Canadian Computer Industry*, Report no. 21, September 1973.

Capre, *Boletim Tecnico*, vol. 1, no. 1, Rio de Janeiro, January/March 1979.

Cardoso, F. H., *Dependency Realised*, Hacket Memorial Lecture, The University of Texas at Austin, 1973.

Cardoso, F. H. and Faletto, *Dependency and Development in Latin America*, University of California Press, Berkeley, Los Angeles and London, 1979.

Carlson, J., 'The Different Modes of Technology Transfer' in Widstrand, C. (ed.), *Multinational Firms in Africa*, Nordiska Afrikainstituted, Uppsala, Sweden, 1975.

Casson, M., *Alternatives to the Multinational Enterprise*, Macmillan, 1979.

Caves, R., 'International Corporation: The Industrial Economics of Foreign Investment', *Economica*, February 1971.

Chudson, W., 'Intra-firm Trade and Transfer Pricing', in Murray, R. (ed.), *Multinationals Beyond the Market*, Harvester Press, 1981.

Computer Weekly, Monthly newspaper on international computer industry, IPC Electrical-Electronic Press Ltd., several issues.

Computer World, International Data Corporation, Mass., USA, several issues.

The Conference Board, *Multinational Corporations and National Élites: A Study in Tensions*, Research Report.

Cooper, C., *Transfer of Technology from Advanced to Developing Countries*, Prepared for UNCTAD, November 1970.

Cooper, C., 'Science Policy and Technological Change in Underdeveloped Economies', *World Development*, vol. 2, no. 3, March 1974.

Cooper, C. and Maxwell, P., *Machinery Supply and the Transfer of Technology to Latin America*, University of Sussex, SPRU, 1975.

Cooper, C., *Policy Interventions for Technological Innovation in Less Developed Countries*, University of Sussex, SPRU, mimeo, 1976.

Cooper, C. and Hoffman, K., *Transactions in Technology and Implications for Developing Countries*, University of Sussex, SPRU, mimeo, 1978.

Cooper, C., 'Aspects of Transfer Pricing in Machinery Markets', Murray, R. (ed.), *Multinationals Beyond the Market*, Harvester Press, 1981.

Cropp, J., Harris, D. and Stern, *Trade in Innovation—The Ins and Outs of Licensing*, Wiley-Interscience, 1970.

Cyert, R. and Mensch, J., *A Behavioural Theory of the Firm*, Prentice-Hall, 1963.

Datamation, Published monthly by Technical Publishing Company, USA. Several issues.

Digibras, *Relatorio Semestral de Marketing*, 1979.

Digibras, *Panorama da Industria Nacional de Computadores e Perifericos*, Brasilia, 1981.

Dosi, G., *Structural Adjustment and Public Policy Under Conditions of Rapid Technical Change: The Semiconductor*, Sussex European Research Centre, University of Sussex, 1980.

Drucker, P., 'Business Objectives and Survival Needs: Notes on a Discipline of Business Enterprise', *The Journal of Business*, vol. 13, no. 2, April 1958.

Dunning, J., *International Investment Selected Readings*, Penguin, 1972.

Dusseldorf Conference on Multinational Corporations, *International Control of Investment*, 1974.

Dymsza, W., *Multinational Business Strategy*, McGraw-Hill, 1972.

Electronics News, Fairchild Business Newspapers, New York, several issues.

Electronics Times, Weekly newspaper for the electronic industry, UK, several issues.

Eqea, A., 'Multinational Corporations in the Operation and Ideology of International Transfer of Technology', *Studies in Comparative International Development*, vol. 10, Spring 1975.

Erber, F. *et al.*, *Assorcao e Criacao de Tecnologia na Industria de Bens de Capital*, FINEP, Serie Pesquisas, no. 2, Rio de Janeiro, 1974.

Erber, F., 'Technological Development and State Intervention: a Study of the Brazilian Capital Goods Industry', University of Sussex, 1977. (D.Phil thesis.)

Evans, P., 'Direct Investment and Industrial Concentration', *Journal of Development Studies*, vol. 13, July 1977.

Evans, P., *Dependent Development: The Alliance of Multinational, State and Local Capital in Brazil*, Princeton Unversity Press, 1979.

Ferrer, A., *Tecnologia y Politica Economica en America Latina*, Editorial Paidos, Buenos Aires, 1974.

Fieldhouse, D. (ed.), *The Theory of Capitalist Imperialism*, Longman, 1967.

Figueiredo, N., *A Transferencia de Tecnologia no Desenvolvimento Industrial do Brasil*, IPEA/INPES, Rio de Janeiro, 1972.

Fortune, *Fortune 300 Directory*, New York, 1975-80.

Foy, N., *The IBM World*, Eyre Methuen Ltd., 1974.

Frank, A., *Lumpen-Bourgeoisie, Lumpen-Development Dependence, Class and Politics in Latin America*, Monthly Review Press, 1972.

Frank, A., *Dependent Accumulation and Underdevelopment*, Macmillan, 1978.

Franko, L., *Joint Venture Survival in Multinational Corporations*, Praeger Publications, New York, 1971.

Freeman, C., *The Economics of Industrial Innovation*, Penguin, 1974.

Freeman, C., 'R & D in Electronic Capital Goods', *National Institute Economic Review*, November 1965.

Fung, S. and Cassiolato, J., *The International Transfer of Technology to Brazil through Technology Agreements—Characteristics of the Government Control System and the Commercial Transactions*, Centre for Policy Alternatives, MIT Press, Cambridge, Mass., 1976.

Gabriel, P., *The International Transfer of Corporate Skills*, Harvard Business School, Cambridge, Mass., 1967.

Galbraith, J. K., *The New Industrial State,* Penguin, 1967, 1972.

Gilpin, R., *Technology, Economic Growth and International Competitiveness*, Subcommittee on Economic Growth of the Joint Economic Committee. Congress of the United States, July 1975.

Globerman, S., 'A Note on Foreign Ownership and Market Structure in the UK', *Applied Economics*, 1979, vol. II, no. 1

Government of Canada, *Foreign Direct Investment in Canada*, Ottawa, 1972.

Gronack, I. and Martin, D., *Managerial Economics, Microeconomic Theory and Firm's Decisions*, Little Brown, Boston, 1973.

Gruber, W. and Marquis, D., (ed.), *Factors in the Transfer of Technology*, MIT Press, Cambridge, Mass., 1969.

Guimaraes, E., 'Industry, Market Structure and the Growth of the Firm in the Brazilian Economy', University College, London, September 1980. (D.Phil thesis.)

Gunneman, J. (ed.), *The Nation State and Transnational Corporations in Conflict*, Praeger, New York, 1975.

Harman, A., *The International Computer Company: Innovation and Competitive Advantage*, Harvard Unversity Press, Cambridge, Mass., 1971.

Hawkins, C., *Theory of the Firm*, Macmillan, 1973.

Helleiner, G. (ed.), *A World Divided: The Less Developed Countries in the International Economy*, Cambridge University Press, 1976.

Helleiner, G., 'Canada and the New International Economic Order', *Canadian Public Policy*, vol. 2, no. 3, Summer 1976.

Hirsch, S., 'The United States Electronic Industry in International Trade', *National Institute Economics Review*, no. 34, 1965.

Hirschman, A., 'The Political Economy of Import Substituting Industrialisation', *Quarterly Journal of Economics*, February 1978.

Holland, S., *Socialist Challenge*, Quartet Books, 1975.

Horowitz, D., *Corporations and the Cold War*, Monthly Review Press, 1969.

Hymer, S., 'The International Operations of National Firms: A Study of Direct Investment', MIT, 1960. (Doctoral thesis.)

Hymer, S., 'The Efficiency (Contradictions) of Multinational Corporations', in Paquet, F. (ed.), *The Multinational Firm and the Nation State*, Collier-Macmillan Canada Ltd., 1972.

Hymer, S., 'The Multinational Corporation and the Law of Uneven Development', in Radice, H. (ed.), *International Firms and Modern Imperialism*, Penguin Modern Economics Readings, 1975.

International Centre for Public Enterprises in Developing Countries (ICPE), *Joint Ventures and Public Enterprises in Developing Countries*, Proceedings of an international seminar held in Ljubljana 4-12 December 1979.

Jequier, N., 'Towards a Technological Policy—the Japanese Model', *Science Policy News*, July 1971.

Jequier, N., 'Computers' in Vernon, R. (ed.), *Big Business and the State: Changing Relations in Wester Europe,* Macmillan, 1974.

Johnson, H., 'The Efficiency and Welfare Implications of the International Corporation', in Kindleberger, C. (ed.), *The International Corporation*, MIT Press, Cambridge, Mass., 1970.

Johnson, H., *Technology and Economic Interdependence*, Macmillan, 1975.

Johnston, R. (ed.), *Directing Technology*, Croom Helm, 1979.

Kaplinsky, R., 'Accumulation and Transfer of Technology: Issues of Conflict and Mechanisms for the Exercise of Control', *World Development*, vol. 4, no. 3, March 1976.

Katz, J., *Importacion de Tecnologia, Aprendizaje Local y Industrialisation Dependiente*, Washington: OAS Programa Regional de Desarollo Cientifico y Tecnologico, 1972.

Katz, J., 'Industrial Growth and R and D', in Urquidi, V. and Thorp, M. (eds.), *Latin America in the International Economy*, Macmillan, 1973.

Katz, J. and Ablin, E., *From Infant Industry to Technology Exports: The Argentine Experience in the International Sale of Industrial Plants and Engineering Works*, UN-ECLA/IDB, Buenos Aires, 1978.

Katz, J., *Domestic Technology Generation in LDCs: A Review of Research Findings*, UN-ECLA, Buenos Aires, 1980.

Katz, J., Technological Change and Development in Latin America, in Ffrench-Davis, R. and Tironi, E. (eds.), *Latin America and the New International Economic Order*, Macmillan Press, 1982.

Kindleberger, C. (ed.), *The International Corporation*, MIT Press, Cambridge, Mass., 1970.

Kindleberger, C., 'The Monopoly Theory of Direct Foreign Investment', Modelski, G. (ed.), *Transnational Corporations and World Order*, W. H. Freeman and Company, San Francisco, 1979.

Kojima, K., *Japan and a New World Economic Order*, Croom Helm, 1977.

Kojima, K., *Direct Foreign Investment: A Japanese Model of Multinational Business Operations*, Croom Helm, 1978.

Lall, S., *Developing Countries as Exporters of Technology and Capital Goods: The Indian Experience*, Oxford University, Institute of Economics and Statistics, mimeo, 1969.

Lall, S. and Streeten, P., *Foreign Investment, Transnationals and Developing Countries*, Macmillan, 1977.

Lall, S., 'Transfer Pricing and Developing Countries: Some Problems of Investigation', *World Development*, vol. 17, no. 1, January 1979.

Lall, S., Developing Countries as Exporters of Industrial Technology, *Research Policy*, vol. 9, no. 1, January 1980.

Lall, S., *Developing Countries as Exporters of Technology,* Macmillan, 1982.

Levitt, K., *Silent Surrender: The Multinational Corporation in Canada*, Macmillan, Toronto, 1971.

Leys, C., Underdevelopment and Dependency: Critical Notes, *Journal of Contemporary Asia*, vol. 7, no. 1, 1977.

Lines, V., *Minicomputer Systems,* Winthrop, Cambridge, Mass., 1980.

MacKintosh Consultants Company Ltd., *Microprocessor/Minicomputer Trends and West European Markets 1975-80*, vol. II, Products, Suppliers and Applications.

MacLean, J., *The Impact of the Microelectronics Industry on the Structure of the Canadian Economy*, Institute for Research on Public Policy, March 1979.

Mansfield, E., *Research and Innovation in the Modern Corporation*, Macmillan, 1972.

Marini, R., 'Dialetica de la Dependencia: La Economia Exportadora', *Socieded y Desarrollo*, vol. 1, no. 1, Santiago, 1972.

Marini, R., 'Brazilian Sub-Imperialism', *Monthly Review*, no. 9, February 1972.

Marques, I., *Computadores: Parte de um caso amplo da sobrevivencia e da soberania nacional*, Rio de Janeiro, 1979.

Marris, R., *The Corporate Economy: Growth, Competition, and Innovative Potential*, Macmillan, 1971.

Martin, D., 'The Computer Industry', Adams, E. (ed.), *The Structure of American Industry*, Macmillan, 1977.

Martins, L., *Nacao e Corporacao Multinacional*, Paz e Terra, Rio de Janeiro, 1975.

Martins, L. C., 'As Perpectivas para o software products' (baseado em palestra realizada no 9° SECOP), *Datanews*, no. 123, July 1981.

Martinez, J., 'O governo no mercado de infomatica', *Dados e Ideias*, vol. 7, no. 3, August 1981.

Marx, K., *Capital*, Vol. I, first published 1867, Lawrence and Wishart, 1977.

Mattelard, A., *Multinational Corporations and the Control of the Culture:*

The Ideological Apparatus of Imperialism, Harvester Press, Brighton, 1979.

Meritt, M., 'Breaking-up of IBM', *The New Scientist,* 6 April 1972.

Merrav, M., *Technological Dependence, Monopoly and Growth,* Pergamon Press, 1969.

Michalet, C., *Transfer of Technology and the Multinational Firm,* OECD, 1973.

Mirow, K., *A Ditadura dos Carteis,* Editora Civilizacao Brasileira, 1977.

Modelski, G. (ed.), *Transnational Corporations and World Order,* W. H. Freeman and Company, San Francisco, 1979.

Murray, R., 'The Internalization of Capital and the Nation State', in Radice, H. (ed.), *International Firms and Modern Imperialism,* Penguin, 1975.

Murray, R., *Transfer Pricing, Multinationals and the State,* University of Sussex, February 1979 (mimeo).

Murray, R. (ed). *Multinationals Beyond the Market,* Harvester Press, 1981.

Myrdal, G., *Asian Drama,* vol. I, Allen Lane, Penguin Press, 1968.

Mytelka, L., 'Licensing and Technology Dependence in the Andean Group', *World Development,* vol. 6, no. 4, April 1978.

Naue, H., *Technology Transfer and US Foreign Policy,* Praeger Publishers, New York, 1976.

Needham, D., 'Market Structure and Firm's R & D Behaviour', *Journal of International Economics,* vol. 23, June 1975.

Newfarmer, R. and Willard, F., *Multinational Corporations in Brazil and Mexico: Structural Sources of Economic and Non-Economic Power.* Report of the Committee of Foreign Relations, US Senate, 1975.

Newfarmer, R., *The International Market Power of Transnational Corporations. A Case Study of the Electrical Industry,* UNCTAD/ST/MD/13, New York, 1978.

Newfarmer, R., *Multinational Conglomerates and the Economies of Dependent Development,* JAI Press, 1979a.

Newfarmer, R., 'Oligopolistic Tactics to Control Markets and the Growth of TNCs in Brazil's Electrical Industry', *The Journal of Development Studies,* vol. 15, no. 3, April 1979b.

Newfarmer, R., 'The Takeovers in Brazil: The Uneven Distribution of Benefit in the Market for Firms' in *World Development* vol. 7, 1979c.

Nora, S. and Minc, A., *L'Informatisation de la Societe,* La Documentation Francaise, Paris, 1978.

OECD, *Gaps in Technology: Electronic Computers,* Paris, 1969.

O'Keefe, W., 'Factors which Contribute to Project Management Difficulties in Brazilian Industrial Research Institute', *Interscience,* vol. 4, no. 2, 1979.

Ozawa, T., *Transfer of Technology from Japan to Developing Countries,* UNITAR, New York, 1981.

Paquet, G., *The Multinational Firm and the Nation State,* Collier-Macmillan Canada Ltd., 1972.

Pavitt, K. and Walker, W., 'Government Policies Towards Industrial Innovation: A Review', *Research Policy 5,* 1976.

Pavitt, K. and Worboys, M., *Science, Technology and the Modern Industrial State,* Butterworths, 1977.

Penrose, E., 'Ownership and Control: MNC in Less Developed Countries', Helleiner, G. (ed.), *A World Divided*, Cambridge University Press, 1976.

Penrose, E., *The Theory of the Growth of the Firm*, Blackwell, 1959.

Penrose, E., *The Growth of Firms, Middle East Oil and Other Essays*, Frank Cass and Co. Ltd., 1971.

Pickering, J., *Industrial Structure and Market Conduct*, Martin Robertson, 1974.

Pipe, R., *Towards Central Government Computer Policy*, OECD (mimeo), 1972.

Radice, H. (ed.), *International Firms and Modern Imperialism*, Penguin Modern Economics Readings, 1975.

Richers, R., *Rumos da America Latina, Desenvolvimento Economico e Mudanca Social*, Blucher, São Paulo, 1976.

Robinson, J., *The Economics of Imperfect Competition*, Macmillan, 1969.

Robinson, R. D., *National Control of Foreign Business Entry: A Survey of Fifteen Countries*, New York, 1976.

Robock, S., *Brazil: A Study in Development Progress*, Lexington Press, 1976.

Rodgers, W., *Think: a Biography of the Watsons and IBM*, Weidenfeld and Nicholson, 1969.

Ronstadt, R., *Research and Development Abroad by US Multinationals*, Praeger Publishers, New York, 1977.

Rosenberg, N., *Perspectives on Technology*, Cambridge University Press, 1976.

Rutenberg, D., 'The Advantages of Being Multinational', in Paquet, F. (ed.), *The Multinational Firm and the Nation State*, Collier-Macmillan, Canada, 1972.

Sagasti, F. and Guerrero, M., *El Desarrollo Cientifico y Tecnologico de America Latina*, Instituto para la Integracion de America Latina, Buenos Aires, 1974.

Salama, P., *O Processo de Subdesenvolvimento*, Vozes, Rio de Janeiro, 1976.

Salter, E., *Productivity and Technical Change*, Cambridge University Press, 1969.

Sandhull, B., *On Product Changes and Product Planning*, SIAR, Lund, Sweden, 1968.

Santos, T., 'El Nuevo Carater de la Dependicia', in Instituto de Estudos Peruanas, *La Cresis del Dessarrollismo y la Nueva Dependencia*, Buenos Aires, 1969.

Santos, T., 'The Crisis of Development Theory and the Problems of Dependency in Latin America', in Benstein, E. (ed.), *Underdevelopment and Development*, Penguin, 1973.

Santos, T., *Imperialismo e Corporacoes Multinacionais*, Paz e Terra, Rio de Janeiro, 1977.

Schumpeter, J., *Business Cycles*, McGraw-Hill, New York, 1939.

Sciberras, E., *Multinational Electronic Companies and National Economic Policies*, JAI Press, 1977.

Sciberras, E., Swords-Isherwood, N. and Senker, P., *Competition, Technical Change and Manpower in Electronic Capital Equipment: A Study of the UK Minicomputer Industry*. SPRU Occasional Paper Series, no. 8, September 1978.

Sciberras, E., *Television and Related Products Sector—Final Report*, OCD, August 1979.

Scott, Goff, Hancock and Co.,—Research Department, *Office Equipment*, June 1975.

Seers, D. (ed.), *Dependency Theory: A Critical Reassessment*, Frances Pinter, 1981.

SEI-Secretaria Especial de Informatica, *Relatorio da Comissao de Software e Servicos*, Brasilia, 1981.

Senker, P. and Swords-Isherwood, N., (eds.), *Microelectronics and the Engineering Industry: The Need for Skills*. Frances Pinter, 1980.

Sercovich, F., *Tecnologia y Control Extrangeiros en la Industria Argentina*, Siglo xxl Editores, Buenos Aires, 1975.

Shepherd, W., *Market Power and Economic Welfare: An Introduction*, Random House, New York, 1970.

Siegel, E., *Non-Parametric Statistical Techniques for the Behavioural Sciences*, London, 1962.

Smith, A., *The Wealth of Nations*, first published in 1776, Pelican, 1970.

Soete, L., 'Inventive Activity, Industrial Organisation and International Trade', University of Sussex, 1978. (D.Phil Thesis.)

Soete, L., Technological Dependency: A Critical View, in Seers, D. (ed.), *Dependency Theory*, Frances Pinter, 1981.

Solomon, L., *Multinational Corporations and the Emerging World Order*, Kennicat Press, 1978.

Staples, E., *Market Structure and Technological Innovation: A Step Towards a Unifying Theory*, College of Business Administration, University of Cincinnati (mimeo), 1976.

Steindl, J. *Maturity and Stagnation in American Capitalism,* Monthly Review Press, New York, 1976.

Stopford, J. and Haberick, K., 'Quantity and Control of Foreign Operations', *Journal of General Management*, vol. 3, no. 4, Summer 1976.

Street, J. and Dilmus, J. (ed.), *Technological Progress in Latin America: The Prospects for Overcoming Dependency*, Westview Press, Boulder, Colorado, 1979.

Sunkel, O., 'Politica Nacional de Desarrollo y Dependencia Externa', *Estudios Internacionales,* no. 1, April 1967.

Sylos-Labini, P., *Oligopoly and Technical Progress,* Harvard University Press, Cambridge, Mass., 1969.

Teixeira, F., 'Intervening Variables in the Process of Accumulation of Technological Capabilities', University of Sussex, 1980. (M.Sc. dissertation.)

Tigre, P., *Industria de Computadores e Dependencia Tecnologica no Brasil*, Coppe/UFRJ, 1978 (Tese de Mestrado).

Tigre, P., 'As Multinacionais da Informatica no Brasil', *Revista de Administracao Publica*, vol. 15, no. 1, January/March 1981.

Tigre, P., 'Brazil: A Future in Homemade Hardware', *South*, UK, February 1982, No. 16, p. 98.

Tomlinson, J., *The Joint Venture Process in International Business: India and Pakistan*, MIT Press, Cambridge, Mass., 1970.

UNCTAD, *Transfer of Technology, Technology Dependence: Its Nature, Consequences and Policy Implications*, December 1975.

UNCTAD, *Electronics in Developing Countries: Issues in Transfer and Development of Technology*, Geneva, 1978.

UN Department of Economics and Social Affairs (DESA), *The Application of Computer Technology for Development*, New York, 1971.

UN DESA, *Multinational Corporations in World Development*, ST/ECA/190, 1973.

UNESCO, Intergovernmental Bureau for Informatics (IBI), *Strategies and Policies for Informatics* (Main Working Document), 1979.

UN Statistical Office, *The Growth of World Industry*, 1975.

Universidade Estadual de Campinas, *Seminario de Ciencia Tecnologia e Estrategia para Independencia*, Duas Cidades, 1977.

US Congress, Committee on the Judiciary, Subcommittee on Antitrust and Monopoly, *Hearings on the Industrial Reorganisation Act: The Computer Industry*, 1974.

US Department of Commerce, *Global Market Survey—Computer Equipment*, October 1973.

US Small Business Administration, *A Study of Small Business in the Electronic Industry*, Washington 23, DC.

Utrecht, E., *Transnational Corporations in South East Asia and the Pacific*, University of Sydney, Transnational Corporations Projects, 1978.

Vaitsos, C., *Transfer of Industrial Technology to Developing Countries through Private Enterprises*, 1970.

Vaitsos, C., 'The Process of Commercialisation of Technology in the Andean Pact' (1971), in Radice, H. (ed.), *International Firms and Modern Imperialism*, Penguin Modern Economics Readings, 1975.

Vaitsos, C., 'Foreign Investment Policies and Economic Development in Latin America', *Journal of World Trade Law*, vol. 7, no. 6, November-December 1973.

Vaitsos, C., *Distribucao de Renda e Empresas Multinacionais*, Paz e Terra, Rio de Janeiro, 1977.

Valdesuso, C., 'Superminis e seu impacto na Politica Nacional de Informatica', *Datanews*, December 1981.

Veliz, C. (ed.), *Obstacle to Change in Latin America*, Oxford University Press, 1975.

Vernon, R. (ed.), *The Technology Factor in International Trade*, National Bureau of Economic Research, New York, 1970.

Vernon, R., *Sovereignty at Bay: The Multinational Spread of US Enterprises*, Basic Books, New York, 1971.

Vernon, R. (ed.), *Big Business and the State*, Macmillan, 1974.

Vernon, R., *Storm over the Multinationals—The Real Issue*, Macmillan, 1977.

Villamil, J. (ed.), *Transnational Capitalism and Rational Development, New Perspectives of Dependence*

Vitteli, G., *Imported Technology and Development of Local Skills*, University of Sussex, 1979 (mimeo).

Von Doellinger, C. and Cavalcanti, L., *Empresas Multinacionais na Industria Brasileira*, IPEA/IMPES, Rio de Janeiro, 1975.

Warren, B., 'Imperialism and Capitalist Industrialisation', *New Left Review*, 81, September/October 1973.

Weinsteing, F., 'Underdevelopment and Efforts to Control Multinational

Corporations', in Modelski, G. (ed.), *Transnational Corporations and World Order*, W. H. Freeman and Company, San Francisco, 1979.

Wilson, R., *The Sale of Technology Through Licensing*, Yale University, 1975.

Wionczek, M. (ed.), *Comercio de Tecnologia y Subdesarollo Economico*, UNAM, Mexico, 1975.

Wionczek, M., *Notes on Technology Transfer Through Multinational Enterprises in Latin America*, February, 1975 (mimeo).

World Market Forecasts (electronic equipment and components) *Electronics International*, McGraw-Hill, January 1981.

Zurawicki, L., *Multinational Enterprises in the West and East*, Sijthoff and Noordhoff, International Publishers (Netherlands), 1979.